COMPOSTING

This book is dedicated to Professor P. H. McGauhey,
my friend and colleague of many years
to whom I owe most of "my" best ideas.

CONTENTS

COMPOSTING

Composting Perspectives— Progress Since 1950

Pre-1950 Period

To broaden the historical perspective of this book, let us delve a bit into the more distant history of composting. To reiterate the timeworn introduction to many a dissertation on composting, it is one of the more ancient of the agricultural arts—and so it remained until the early 1900's when Sir Albert Howard (1) began to systematize the traditional compost procedures. His collaborators were F. K. Jackson and Y. D. Wad. As any organic devotee knows, the system developed by Sir Albert became known as the Indore system—i.e., it was named after that region of India in which it was developed.

Immediately preceding Sir Albert's work and for a time thereafter, the major non-agricultural interest in composting outside of the U.S. was the use of the method as a means of treating night-soil in those regions lacking sewerage facilities. As such, the concern was more in using composting as a hygienic measure than as a conservation measure, although conservation was offered as an added incentive. Thus, while Sir Albert was interested in both aspects of composting, the possibility of treating night-soil in a hygienic manner was a major incentive to his efforts. Another early worker who applied composting to the treatment of night-soil was Van Vuren. (2) Both workers relied on reduction of fly-breeding as a parameter of hygienic quality.

1950—Early 1960 Period

The 1940's and the early 1950's marked the beginning of a surge of interest in the use of composting as a means of reclaiming plant nutrients in municipal refuse, and thereby as a solid waste "disposal" process. The term "disposal" is used in the popular sense, namely processing the wastes after they have been collected and concentrated at a designated site.)

Research

It was at that time that a need began to be felt for undertaking studies to develop the scientific principles of composting and to bring some order and shed some light upon the welter of folk-lore and superstition that characterized the practice until that time. Thus, research conducted by the New Zealand Government's Inter-Departmental Committee for the Disposal of Organic Wastes led to the publication of two reports in which were explored the scientific aspects of the mechanics of the soil improvement accomplished by incorporating compost in the soil. (3) It was also at this time that the University of California began its research on composting, an outcome of which was technical bulletin no. 9, "Reclamation of Municipal Refuse by Composting" (4). This publication contained the first formal enunciation of the scientific principles of composting; and interpreted them in a form directly applicable to the development of a rational technology. The U.S. Public Health Service of Department of Health, Education, and Welfare became actively involved in research and pilot scale studies in the late 1950's and early 1960's (5, 6). This work led to a further refinement of the principles developed at the University of California and New Zealand.

The efforts of European researchers during this period were largely oriented towards the hygienic aspects of composting. While the U.S. researchers were concerned about the survival of pathogenic organisms, they did little actual experimentation on the subject. On the other hand, research by several European workers involved actual observations on the survival of selected pathogens under a variety of conditions in composting (7, 8). In general, their results confirmed the predictions of the U.S. researchers,

2

although the required durations of exposure proved to be somewhat longer.

Among the specific fundamentals for composting municipal refuse and large-scale agricultural operations found to exist by the researchers during the 1950 and early 1960 period were the following: 1) For aesthetic and hygienic reasons, the composting process should be aerobic, at least to the extent that no malodorous reduced intermediate products develop. 2) It should be thermophilic during a significant portion of the process. Obtaining thermophilic conditions requires no input of external energy if the composting mass is sufficiently insulated, and biologically oriented environmental conditions are appropriate. 3) No inoculation with external microbial cultures is necessary either before, during, or after the composting process. This fact was demonstrated repeatedly at the major research centers. 4) The relations between the environmental factors and the course of the process, not unexpectedly, were shown to be those characteristic of any biological process. As a corollary, the futility was demonstrated of trying to arrive at absolute (i.e., universally applicable) values for *operational* factors inasmuch as these will vary with the nature of the material to be composted and the type of equipment used in composting. 5) Unless economically unrealistic methods are used, composting of municipal and large scale agricultural wastes is a relatively slow process, i.e. a matter of two or more weeks before the material is sufficiently stabilized to be stored without giving rise to a nuisance.

Technology and Status

The advent of the concept of using composting as a means of treating municipal wastes sparked a flurry of activity directed towards the development of constantly increasingly complicated mechanical devices for containing the compost process. Note the use of the word "contain." The term is used because in many cases, the wastes were

3

composted despite being contained in a mechanical device. This hurry to develop mechanical devices finally reached a level at which overmechanization became as much a threat to the cause of composting as any other factor.

Probably the crux of the problem of over-mechanization was twofold—the naiveté of the public with respect to composting, and the perspicacity of the promoter in seizing upon the possibility of using the public interest in conservation to making a "quick dollar." The result was that emphasis was placed upon equipment rather than upon the process itself. The problem was further aggravated on a somewhat lesser scale, monetarily speaking, by the purveyors of inoculums. In some cases, the equipment manufacturer hoped to amplify the financial returns from the sale of his equipment by selling with it a supply of inoculum. An interesting feature of the sales promotions for the inoculums was the parallel between time of appearance of names of microorganisms reported in the literature and that of those advertised in the sales literature.

The combination of over-mechanization and over-promotion led to the development of some of the difficulties that have hindered the successful widespread use of composting as a solid waste "disposal" method in this country. Two of these difficulties were: 1) an excessive optimism in terms of regarding composting as a panacea for the solid waste management woes in this country; and 2) the establishment of a double standard whereby the success of composting is measured on the basis of financial returns from the sales of the product; whereas other "disposal" processes are judged solely by their effect on the environment. These two developments were the inevitable outcome of sales promotions that promised to convert wastes to a readily salable product in a few short days, in a manner completely innocuous to the environment.

Lest the reader gain the impression that all technology and entrepreneurs were of the ilk described above, it should be pointed out, that this period marked the development of reliable equipment and mechanized processes. Among these were the University of California windrow process.

This method is best suited to small scale operations and in countries where labor is plentiful and inexpensive. The Dano and the Naturizer systems are two others that come to mind. Another process that should not be overlooked is the V.A.M. process which has been practiced in Holland since 1932.

Mid-1960 Period

Research on composting received a considerable impetus in the mid-1960's both as a result of funds made available through the passage of the 1965 Solid Wastes Act, and of a beginning of concern of the public for its environment. The research was characterized in large part by the rediscovery of the findings made by the early researchers. Perhaps the most unfortunate part of this period of "rediscovery" was that in many instances the new "discoverers" were unaware of the findings of their predecessors. The major difference between the two groups was that the reports of the latter were couched in a more sophisticated terminology than were the earlier works which contained all of the usual "fad words."

No sizable advances were made in compost technology. Changes that were made, were mostly modifications of earlier systems. One departure from the usual, was the Fairfield Hardy digester, whereas, other systems relied upon tumbling for aeration—whether it be by means of a rotating drum, dropping from one level to another, or by a traveling endless belt. In the Fairfield Hardy system aeration is provided by rotating hollow perforated augers through the composting mass. Air is blown through the augers and enters the wastes from the perforations as the augers rotate in and are being rotated through the mass.

Unfortunately, the mid-1960 period was marred by a succession of financial failures of compost plants. In fact the economic picture became so bleak for composting as a municipal waste treatment process, that only the far-sightedness and dedication of a few kept the interest in composting from disappearing entirely. It did have the beneficial effect

5

of discouraging and weeding out those promoters who were solely concerned with a quick and exorbitant return on their investment. It also was beneficial in that it paved the way for a truly realistic approach to the use of composting as a solid waste management procedure.

Late 1960's to the Present

The late 1960's not only brought a deepening public concern with preserving the quality of the environment, but also a wilingness to do something about it. This concern and willingness persists despite political and industry-generated attempts to discourage both trends. One of the spin-offs of this renewed concern with conservation and the environment is a renewed interest in composting. For one thing, the fallacy of the "double-standard" has been abandoned, and now the idea of composting as a paying proposition in a purely monetary sense has been practically universally abandoned. Instead, the process is being evaluated in terms of its complete social benefits. For example, the transition has been made from the point at which the worth of the compost product was judged primarily upon the dollar-and-cents value of its nitrogen, phosphorus, and potassium (NPK) content. Now, the NPK monetary value of compost has been recognized for what it is—quite minor in terms of environment betterment and improvement of soil quality. Maximum productivity of the soil is the proper criterion—not a balance between cash value of increased crop production per dollar spent on the NPK needed to bring about the increase. Thus, the effect of the compost product on the lasting improvement of the soil is receiving its due attention. Another application beginning to receive attention is that of incorporating compost into the soil to prevent nitrogen contamination of ground waters by converting it (nitrogen) into a relatively insoluble form, namely, microbial protoplasm. The nitrogen is released in a gradual manner through the death and decay of the microbes. Attention was focused on this desirable trend as a result of the growing alarm over the increasing contamination of our water supply attending the excessive use of inorganic nitrogen fertilizers in large-scale agriculture.

A need (and hence a use) for the compost product is being recognized in the repairing of the great damage done to the environment by man in his exploitation of the mineral and coal resources of the earth—e.g., the practice of strip mining. By covering the gouged earth with a layer of compost, there is at least some hope of restoring the despoiled areas to a semblance of their former condition.

Research activity on composting—at least in the U.S.— has dwindled to practically nothing. However, this is not quite the disaster one would suppose, inasmuch as a great deal of the so-called recent research had been a repetition of that done by the "pioneers." Nevertheless, there do remain areas in need of further study. Some examples are as follows: 1) survival of viruses; 2) fate of heavy metals; 3) long-term effect on the soil, and hence ultimately on crops; and 4) more about the true economics of composting.

The technology is more than adequate as far as the composting process itself is concerned. However, there is room for improvement in the technologies involved in pretreatment steps, especially sorting and grinding. Time does not permit a detailed or even a cursory discussion of the state-of-the-art of automatic sorting. Suffice it to state that the only existing reliable methods are hand-sorting and the magnetic separation for the ferrous metals. Although great strides have been made in grinding technology, the problems of abrasion and high capital and operating costs continue to be problem areas.

The subject of technology should not be concluded without saying a few words about a machine, the use of which should result in a distinct betterment of the economics of composting. It is the Terex-Cobey 74-51 Composter. The news item in the column "Organic World" of the May issue of the magazine *Organic Gardening* is an excellent summation of the advantages coming from the use of the machine. The machine is rather simply designed; it is mobile; and reasonably priced in view of its capacity, thus making capital and operating costs low. It is backed by an obviously well-capitalized organization, namely General Motors.

In conclusion, it can be stated that: 1) The unfavorable economics of composting, both real and apparent, can be made more favorable—the former by relying less upon highly mechanized installations; and the latter, by considering all factors when comparing composting costs with those of disposal processes other than sanitary landfill. 2) Attention should be given to the potential of composting solid wastes management for the smaller cities, inasmuch as access may be had more readily to the nitrogenous wastes needed to compost modern urban refuse. (Composting is not a magical process, it is bound by the same nutritional requirements, especially carbon and nitrogen (C/N ratio), as is any other biological process.) 3) Finally, the more ardent proponents of composting should drop their defensive posture as betrayed by their tendency to classify any system other than composting as being *ipso facto* evil. It should always be remembered that only about 50% of the wastes of a municipality are compostable,—or even burnable. Hence, a sizable fraction of the waste stream can have but one destiny, namely the landfill. Often by being unduly critical of a competing method one leaves himself wide-open to charges of ignorance, and thereby lessens the effectiveness of his advocacy of his own system. An example is a statement to the effect that all sanitary landfills produce leachates. On the contrary, a well-designed sanitary landfill does not produce a leachate. A more valid criticism would be that much of value in wastes is buried and lost in a landfill. Similarly to state that incineration and air pollution are synonymous would be an erroneous statement, since the air pollution from a modern well-designed incinerator can be insignificant. On the other hand, when they were operating, the compost plants at Phoenix (Arizona) in San Fernando (California), and in Florida often were plagued with odor problems. The real criticism of incineration is that it results in the destruction of reclaimable resources. A far better approach is to stress the benefits of

8

composting and to concentrate on seeing to it that composting is practiced where it can serve a need.

References

1. Howard, Albert. "The Manufacture of Humus by the Indore Process." *J. Royal Soc. Arts, 84:*25 (1935).
2. Van Vuren, J.P.J. "Soil Fertility and Sewage." Faber, London, (236 pp.) (1949).
3. "Utilization of Organic Wastes." Second Interim Report of the Interdepartmental Committee on Utilization of Organic Wastes. *New Zealand Engineering. Vol. 6,* Numbers 11 to 12 (November–December 1951).
4. McGauhey, P. H., and C. G. Golueke. "Reclamation of Municipal Refuse by Composting." Tech. Bull. No. 9. Sanit. Eng. Res. Lab., University of California, Berkeley, (June 1953) (Out-of-print).
5. Maier, P. P., E. R. Williams, and G. P. Mallison. "Composting Studies I—Composting Municipal Refuse by the Aeration Bin Process." Reprint No. 277 from *Engineering Bulletin,* Proceedings of the 12th Industrial Waste Conference, Series No. 94, 13-15 May 1953. U.S. Dept. Health, Education, and Welfare.
6. Wiley, J. G. "Composting Studies II—Progress Report on High-Rate Composting Studies." Reprint No. 237 from *Engineering Bulletin,* Proc. of the 12th Industrial Waste Conf., Series No. 94, 13-15 May 1957. U.S. Dept. Health, Education, and Welfare.
7. Knoll, K. H. "Composting From the Hygienic Viewpoint." Intern. Res. Group on Refuse Disposal. English translation by U.S. Dept. Health, Education, and Welfare. IRGR Information Bull. 7, p. 10, July 1959.
8. Parrakova, E. "Hygienic Criteria of the Evaluation of Refuse Compost." Intern. Res. Group on Refuse Disposal, English translation by U.S. Dept. Health, Education, and Welfare. IRGR Information Bulletin 16, p. 10, December 1962.

PART I.

Principles

Principles

Abstract

Composting is a biological process for converting organic solid wastes into a stable, humus-like product whose chief use is as a soil conditioner. Modern composting is aerobic and combines mesophilic and thermophilic temperatures. As a biological process it is subject to the constraints of all biological activities, i.e., limitations imposed by microbial population and genetic traits, and by environmental factors. Costs are comparable to those for incineration.

Definition

Simply stated, composting is the biological decomposition of the organic constituents of wastes under controlled conditions. The term "decomposition" is used instead of "stabilization", because when applied in practical usage, the process rarely is carried on to the point at which the waste is completely stabilized. In fact, the cut-off point may at times be short of "temporary stabilization". The term "biological" distinguishes composting from other types of decomposition, such as chemical or physical (e.g., incineration, pyrolysis, etc.). "Organic" is applicable because, with few exceptions, only the organic portion of wastes is subject to biological breakdown. A very important term in the definition is "controlled". It is the application of control that distinguishes composting from the natural rotting, putrefaction, or other decomposition, that takes place in an open dump, a sanitary landfill, in a manure heap, in an open field, etc.

Classification

Compost systems can be classified on three general bases, namely, oxygen usage, temperature, and technological approach. If oxygen usage is the basis, the division is into aerobic and anaerobic. When temperature serves as the basis, the division becomes mesophilic and thermophilic. Finally, using technology as the key, the classification is into open or windrow and mechanical or "enclosed" composting. The terms in each of the classifications are practically self-explanatory.

Aerobic composting involves the activity of aerobic microbes, and hence the provision of oxygen during the composting process. The opposite prevails in anaerobic composting—i.e., anaerobic bacteria accomplish the decomposition and oxygen (air) is excluded from the composting mass. Aerobic composting generally is characterized by high temperatures, the absence of foul odors, and is more rapid than anaerobic composting. Anaerobic decomposition is characterized by low temperatures (unless heat is applied from an external source), the production of odorous intermediate (reduced) products, and generally proceeds at a slower rate than does aerobic composting. The advantages of aerobic composting over anaerobic composting arise from the differences in their characteristics—in other words, aerobic composting is more rapid, permits high temperatures, and is not odorous. The main advantage in anaerobic composting is that the process can be carried on with a minimum of attention, and as such it can be sealed from the environment. Because of its many advantages, most modern compost processes are basically aerobic—or attempt to be.

As the term implies, in mesophilic composting the temperatures are kept at intermediate temperatures ($15°$ to $40°C$), which in most cases is the ambient temperature. Thermophilic composting is conducted at temperatures from $45°C$ to $65°C$. In practice, most processes include the two ranges.

Compost systems falling under the category of "open" or "windrow" are those in which the entire process is carried out in the open. The manner of arranging the material for handling or processing usually is to stack the materials in elongated windrows. In mechanical systems, on the other hand, the greater part of the initial composting activity takes place in an enclosed unit, the digester. More complete descriptions and a discussion of the respective advantages and disadvantages of the two approaches are given later in this chapter. It might be pointed out at this time that most mechanical processes involve windrowing towards the end of the process to allow the composting material "to mature."

General Constraints Due to Biological Nature

A point of major importance in designing and planning and evaluating a compost process as a waste management device is that since it is a biological operation, factors and requirements peculiar to the maintenance of biological activities in general also affect the compost process. Therefore, composting is subject to well defined biological limitations which are: 1) A suitable microbial population must be present; 2) The rate and efficiency of the process are functions of the rate and efficiency of microbial activity; 3) The capacity of a given operation is limited by the size and nature of the microbial population; 4) The substrate subject to composting generally must be organic; 5) Environmental factors are of key importance.

The origin of the first constraint is quite obvious and is implied in the definition itself of composting. Since the process is a biological one, living organisms are the agents for accomplishing it. The limitation to microbial organisms is indirectly implied by the term "decomposition," in that in nature, decomposition in the commonly accepted sense of the term is done by microscopic organisms. Not only must a microbial population be present, but it must also be one that is suited to the task.

The limitation on rate is one of practical importance, because it means that no matter how well a piece of compost equipment is designed mechanically, composting with it will proceed at a pace commensurate with that of the bacterial activity permitted by the particular set of conditions provided by the machine. The microbial limitation on capacity also has practical ramifications. It means that once the maximum-sized microbial population has been reached under the conditions provided by a given piece

15

of compost equipment, the loading can not be increased without giving rise to nuisances. Loading in excess of the maximum permissible will inhibit the process either partly or entirely, and at the least will result in only partial treatment of the waste material.

The constraint arising from the influence of environmental factors usually manifests itself through the mechanism of the limiting factor. If any factor is present in less than optimum concentration or level, the functioning of the entire process is inhibited in proportion to the extent of the deficiency of the factor. For example, for a given set-up in which the temperature is optimum, aeration is complete, and a suitable microbial population is present, but nitrogen is deficient, the only way to increase the efficiency of that set-up would be to add nitrogen in an amount sufficient to make up for the nitrogen deficiency. Adding more bacteria would only aggravate the problem, since the nitrogen is not sufficient even for the existing population. Building a more elaborate digester would not suffice, since the effective component of the process, namely the bacteria, do not have the nitrogen to meet their metabolic requirements.

Microbiology

Utility of Isolates

Before considering the identity of microbial groups to be found in composting material, a few words of caution are in order. In general, it can be safely stated that there is an overall aura of futility in attempts to isolate and identify all of the organisms to be found in a mass of composting material, at least down to species or even genus. The reasons are many. An important one is the difficulty— bordering on the impossible—of knowing for sure that an isolate is the correct one or is an "artifact" due to the isolation technique. By "artifact" here is meant the isolation of an organism or organisms other than the sought-for one. Such an event could occur through the use of a medium not suitable to the organisms or organisms most responsible for the breakdown. By the same token, simply because a particular group is isolated in greater numbers than other groups does not mean that it is actually more numerous than the others; and certainly it is no proof that it is the most active. The nature of the medium is not the only factor in promoting the error, the lack of interaction of other types of microorganisms in an isolation culture is of importance. The absence of competition under the isolation conditions combined with the use of a favorable medium can enable an organism to flourish, which in a compost pile actually exerts only an insignificant effect on the process. In fact, most of the isolation procedures are at least in part enrichment techniques or modifications thereof to encourage the growth of one organism at the expense of others.

Granted that one could be assured that he has correctly identified the organisms in a given compost heap and has unmistakenly assigned a proper role to each of the isolates, he has no assurance that the same overall microbiological set-up would exist in another operation in a different locale. A number of factors could occur to bring about a difference. The type and proportions of the wastes in the second operation could differ. This would mean the existence of a different substrate and hence a different population composition. Physical conditions could differ—e.g., the moisture content may be significantly higher, the ambient temperature lower, etc. Another possibility is that the indigenous populations may differ.

An answer that might be made to the question of the utility of isolating and identifying the organisms is that if one knows of the identity of the important microorganisms in a compost pile, he can determine the optimum growth conditions for them as well as their growth kinetics by way of pure culture. With this information at hand, he can design the plant and operation accordingly. The rebuttal to the answer is that as far as determining the optimum growth conditions is concerned, all one learns from pure culture studies is the nature of the optimum set of conditions for a given organism in an "artificial situation," which may or may not be the same as that which prevails during the compost process in which interaction with other organisms is an important factor. In other words, the ecology in the actual application is not taken into consideration. Furthermore, the optimum conditions for the key organisms in their "natural" environment, i.e., in the compost pile, can be more readily and more accurately determined by working with the material as it comes with its indigenous microbial population. The criterion for optimality then would be that set of conditions at which decomposition proceeds most rapidly and in the desired manner. This can be done without identifying a single organism. The resulting set of conditions would represent the integration of all factors *in situ*.

INOCULA

The preceding discussion leads to another consideration, namely, the question of the utility of inoculums. Occasionally, a proposal for commercial composting includes the use of some special inoculum, the composition of which is known only to the discoverer who claims it to be fundamental to the successful operation of his process. Some inoculums are described as mixtures of several pure strains of laboratory cultured organisms especially prominent in the decomposition of organic matter and in nitrogen fixation. Others are purported to contain as well such things as "enzyme systems," "hormones," "preserved living organisms," "activated factors," "biocatalysts,' etc.

The idea of inoculation has even been carried to the extent of inoculation of the finished compost. The addition of organisms is supposed to be of inestimable value to the soil. While it is true that certain bacteria promote soil fertility, the mere addition of such organisms is of no use if environmental conditions are not appropriate in the soil. On the other hand, if environmental conditions are suitable, the addition of the organisms would be superfluous because the native population would already be present in more than ample numbers (1).

The number of bacteria is rarely a limiting factor in composting, since bacteria are always present in great abundance on all exposed objects, especially on municipal refuse. They can be eliminated only by a drastic measure such as sterilization at high temperature and pressure. When environmental factors are appropriate, native bacteria, because they are better adapted than forms attenuated under laboratory conditions, multiply rapidly and composting proceeds at a rate governed by the environmental conditions. The vast number of enzymes involved in decomposition, as well as the difficulty and expense involved in isolating and synthesizing them, would make composting with enzymes alone highly impractical even were such a preparation available. The addition of enzymes to raw refuse is unnecessary however, because bacteria synthesize efficiently and rapidly all of the enzymes required. For a time, "hormones' served as the "catch" word and was popularly used to designate growth factors and vitamins needed by bacteria. However, the organic constituents of refuse contain all the growth factors and vitamins needed for normal growth.

Inoculation would be of value to the composting process only if the bacterial population in any emerging environment were unable to develop rapidly enough to take full advantage of the capacity of the environment to support it. In such a case, a time lag would result, which could be overcome by supplementing the initial population indigenous to the refuse. No such time lag was observed in composting studies conducted at the University of California. Composting is a dynamic process, representing the combined activity of a wide succession of mixed bacterial and fungal populations associated with a wide succession of environments, one overlapping the other and each emerging gradually as a result of continual change in temperature and substrate. The substrate changes are due to a progressive breakdown by bacteria of complex foodstuffs to increasingly simple compounds. As will be seen later, temperature increases steadily in proportion to biological activity, so that initial mesophilic conditions are soon superseded by thermophilic ones. Because the process is dynamic and any individual group of organisms can survive in a rather wide environmental range, one population begins to emerge while another is flourishing, and yet another is disappearing. Inasmuch as any group of bacteria is capable of multiplying at a pace equal to that of its developing environment, the addition of similar organisms as an inoculum would be superfluous.

In the University of California studies, the composting process was neither accelerated nor the final product improved in those runs in which inoculums were tested, even though the inoculums were rich in bacteria. Inoculums that were tried were horse manure, "rich" soils, composting material, and two commercial preparations. The University findings have been duplicated at several other laboratories.

In closing this discussion on inoculums, a distinction should be made between inoculation in terms of microbiological research and that in sanitary engineering practice. The difference between the two interpretations is one of magnitude. The microbiologist usually thinks of inoculation as minute additions; whereas the sanitary engineer thinks of what may be described as "mass inoculation." Although the preceding discussion was concerned primarily with inoculation in terms of microbiological usage, it also is applicable to mass inoculation provided the magnitude of the mass inoculum is not such as to *significantly affect the physical and chemical characteristics of the mass of material* receiving the inoculum. Any apparent improvement following a large mass inoculation cannot be attributed solely to the addition of organisms inasmuch as such an inoculation may also significantly alter the physical and chemical nature of the material to be composted.

Types of Microorganisms

Despite the constraints and discouraging situation described in the two preceding subsections, and because of the scientific curiosity present in true researchers, considerable effort has been expended in identifying organisms found in composting materials. In the various studies, certain groups of microorganisms have been found to be apparently associated with different stages of the process.

In the University of California studies (3), facultative and obligate aerobic representatives of bacteria, fungi, and actinomycetes were encountered. (Although strictly speaking, the actinomycetes are higher forms of bacteria, they are treated separately from other bacteria in this discussion because of their distinct role in the compost process.) Bacteria were characteristically predominant at the start of the process, with fungi appearing in 7 to 10 days, and actinomycetes becoming conspicuous only in the final stages. Bacteria were found in all parts of a pile (the windrow method was used in the studies), whereas actinomycetes and fungi were confined to a sharply defined outer zone two to five inches in thickness, beginning just under the surface of the pile. In most cases, the population of fungi and actinomycetes was great enough to impart a distinctly grayish-white appearance to this zone. The limitation of these two groups to the outer zone probably was a function either of temperature or of aeration, or of both. The temperature range of the zone was from 48°C up to 58°C. This range corresponds to that of *Actinomyces thermophilus* established by Gilbert as between 45°C and 60°C (9) and by Miehe as between 40°C and 60°C (10). Among the actinomycetes noted, both *Streptomyces* and *Micromonospora* were recognized, with *Micromonospora* being the more common. Forsyth (11) noted a similar predominance of *Micromonospora* in his work with grass composts. Fungi observed in the studies included *Thermomyces* spp, *Penicillium dupontii*, and *Aspergillus fumigatus*. In more recent research carried on in Britain, workers at the University of Cambridge isolated seventeen types of fungi from compost (12). Among the isolates were *Chaetomium thermophile, Humicola lanuginosa, Talaromyces duponti,* and *Mucor pusillus*. Regan and Jeris (13) in a review of the literature on the decomposition of cellulose and refuse write of *Vibrio napi,* and *V. prima, Occuspora,* sp, *Monosporium* sp, *Mycogone nigra, Botryosporium* sp, and *Stactybotrys* sp.

Substrate (nutrients)

NATURE

The nature of the substrate in composting obviously is that of the wastes being processed. As implied in the definition, the waste, with rare exception, must be organic. Of course, as stated earlier "organic" in the chemical sense covers a multitude of materials. In terms of composting, it refers mostly to "organic" as interpreted in the popular sense, e.g., to paper, wood, manures, food preparation wastes, crop wastes, etc. In terms of microbial nutrition, all of these forms are highly complex substances, and thus are not available to a large number of groups of microbes. It is only as the materials are decomposed to simpler and yet more simple forms that the spectrum of potential microbial users broadens. The course of breakdown for the protein content is: Protein→peptides→amino acids→ammonium compounds→bacterial protoplasm and atmospheric nitrogen or ammonia. Of course, this outline of breakdown is highly abbreviated and does not take into consideration the many possible intermediates and side reactions. For instance, each step actually is accompanied by the synthesis of bacterial protoplasm, inasmuch as when an organism decomposes a substrate, some of the nitrogen is transformed into protoplasm. The following scheme for the complex carbonaceous part of the substrate also is oversimplified: Carbohydrate→simple sugars→organic acids→CO_2 and bacterial protoplasm.

An important feature of a substrate as far as composting is concerned is the availability of the nutrients tied up in the substrate to the microorganisms. Thus, as indicated in the preceding paragraph, the carbon in the raw wastes might just as well not be there as far as the greater part of the indigenous population is concerned, simply because in its existing form, the carbon cannot be assimilated. Therefore, if the first members of the microbial succession were missing, nothing much would happen. However, as stated in the section on inoculation, such an event rarely happens; and to paraphrase a biblical remark, refuse carries the seeds of its own destruction. The important point is that the simpler the form in which the waste occurs, the wider the array of bacterial species to which it is subject to attack— and hence the more rapid the pace at which composting proceeds. Consequently, vegetable trimmings from a supermarket compost much more rapidly than does straw or sawdust.

NUTRIENT BALANCE

To keep on reproducing and thus bring about decomposition, all microorganisms, indeed all organisms, must have a minimum supply of all of the elements of which their cellular matter is composed. In addition, they need a minimum amount of certain elements that enter into the metabolic activities of the organisms as an energy source or enzyme constituent and do not necessarily contribute to an increase in the mass of the organisms. As one knows almost intuitively, the amounts required vary from element to element, and at a somewhat constant ratio of one to another. In other words, a balance is struck. The balance arises from the fact that, as stated earlier, growth is limited by that factor (or factors) which is (or are) present in less than the required concentration. The balance is especially important as far as the macronutrients are concerned. (Macronutrients are those required in relatively large amounts—e.g., carbon and nitrogen.)

One of the more important balances with respect to composting is the carbon-nitrogen balance or ratio (C/N ratio). Because part of the carbon is lost as CO_2; and depending upon the type of organism, carbon is present in the cellular material in greater concentration than is nitrogen, the amount of carbon required considerably surpasses that of nitrogen.

The optimum range with most wastes falls within 20 or 25 to 1. The more the carbon-nitrogen balance deviates from the optimum, especially in the upper range, the slower the process proceeds. However, the actual upper limit for an individual application depends upon the degree of availability of the carbon. If the carbon is present in a form highly resistant to bacterial attack, it is of little use to microbes. Hence, if a waste has a large percentage of carbon in a resistant form, the permissible carbon-nitrogen ratio can be higher than 25/1. Examples are wastes having a heavy concentration of paper, fiber, wood, or straw.

The nitrogen concentration of a sample of the refuse to be composted can be determined by the usual Kjeldahl method. If access to equipment for carbon analysis is not available, the carbon content can be roughly determined according to a formula developed by New Zealand researchers (14) in the 1950's. The formula is as follows:

$$\% \text{ carbon} = \left(\frac{100 - \% \text{ ash}}{1.8} \right)$$

In the University of California studies it was found that the results of this method approximated the more accurate laboratory determination of carbon within 2 to 10%.

Modern municipal wastes generally have a nitrogen content too low for best, or even practical, composting. The reason is simple, very few food products reach the "garbage" can. The packaging of foods has cut down the amount of food-related wastes generated at the home; and that which is generated there, is ground to the sewers. The nitrogen deficiency can be made up by adding nitrogenous wastes such as manures and digested sewage sludge.

The principal deleterious effect of too low a C/N ratio is the loss of nitrogen through the production of ammonia and its subsequent volatilization. Apparently, the excess nitrogen ends up as ammonia. As far as the composting process is concerned *per se*, such an event is not detrimental. But since nitrogen conservation should be one of the objectives of composting, the loss becomes significant on that score. The loss is greatest when high-rate composting is being employed. The increased loss is due to the fact that high-rate composting involves a great deal of aeration, is generally occurring under thermophilic conditions, and is characterized by a pH level of 8.0 or above. The high pH fosters ammonia formation; the high temperature accelerates the volatilization of ammonia, and the aeration drives off the volatilized ammonia. While the factors involved in the volatilization may suggest the remedy, applying the remedy may not be practical. For example, the pH could be lowered by adding some type of acid. Of course such a procedure would be impractical from the standpoint of processing and expense. Without aeration, the process no longer is high-rate composting. The temperature could be lowered, but this would only reduce the rate of loss, and not necessarily the total amount of loss. Consequently, the most appropriate approach is to avoid the low carbon-nitrogen ratios if possible.

Rate Controlling Factors

GENERAL

Since the compost process is essentially a biological one, rate controlling factors in the process are those influencing biological activity in general, namely, environmental factors. In fact, organism-related factors are perhaps the ultimate rate limiting factors, because they determine the rate of growth and degree of activity of the microbial population, and hence the rapidity and nature of the compost process. The principal environmental factors in composting are moisture, temperature, pH level (hydrogen ion concentration), nutrient concentration and availability, and oxygen concentration.

Nutrient concentration is not discussed in this section because it was given sufficient consideration in the previous section.

MOISTURE CONTENT

The theoretical optimum moisture content in composting is 100%. The practical moisture content, however, is a function of aeration capacity of the process equipment and of the structural nature of the material being composted. From the strictly biological point of view, the ideal arrangement would be to slurry the refuse and then to vigorously bubble air through the slurry at a rate at which the slurry would be completely aerobic, much like the conventional activated sludge process in sewage treatment. Because of technological and economic reasons, the aerated slurry approach is impractical for most waste composting applications.

The usual practice has been to resort to "dry" handling in composting, i.e., the material is not suspended in water. With this type of handling—in other words—with composting in general, the structural strength of the material to be composted determines the upper permissible moisture content. The relation between structure and moisture content stems from the fact that modern composting is an aerobic process. Oxygen is made available to the bacteria by way of the air contained in the interstices at the time the windrow was formed. In a mechanical composter, the supply is by way of the air introduced between the particles as they are tumbled or stirred in the digester. In either case, if the interstices are filled with water, obviously the air has been displaced and no oxygen is available to the organisms. As a result, the mass of waste becomes anaerobic and the composting process is slowed and foul odors are generated. The size of the interstices is determined by the particle size of the material, and their stability is determined by the structural strength of the composting material—i.e., the capacity to resist compaction and consequent obliteration of the interstices.

Inasmuch as a 100% moisture content is the desideratum, the maximum permissible moisture content *ipso facto* becomes the optimum moisture for a given material. The maximum permissible moisture contents for various wastes are listed in Table I.

As the table indicates, the maximum permissible moisture content for composting wastes that are largely "fibrous" (straw, hay, dry leaves, etc.) or woody (sawdust, small wood chips, bark, etc.) is within the range of 75 to 85% (13). On the other hand, wastes consisting mostly of paper

TABLE I

MAXIMUM PERMISSIBLE MOISTURE CONTENTS

Type of Waste[a]	Moisture Content %
Theoretical	100
Straw	75-85
Wood (sawdust, small chips)	75-90
Paper	55-65
"Wet" Wastes (vegetable trimmings, lawn clippings, garbage, etc.)	50-55
Municipal Refuse	55-65
Manures (without bedding)	55-65

[a] The major component of the waste.

or of green vegetation (lawn clippings, vegetable trimmings, wet garbage, etc.) have a maximum permissible moisture content within the range of 50% to 60%. If the maximum permissible moisture content for a given waste is excessively low, the problem can be lessened by adding an absorbent waste to the material. Thus, if straw is added to vegetable trimmings, the maximum permissible moisture rises in proportion to the amount of straw added. The addition of an absorbent also is required if the moisture content of the waste in its "raw" state is excessively high, as for example cannery wastes.

The minimum moisture content at which bacterial activity takes place is from 12 to 15%. Obviously, the closer the moisture content of a composting mass approaches these low levels, the slower will be the compost process. As a rule-of-thumb, the moisture content becomes a limiting factor when it drops below 45 or 50% (3, 10).

TEMPERATURE

Temperature has long been recognized as one of the key environmental factors affecting biological activity. In general, each group of organisms has an optimum temperature, and any deviation from the optimum is manifested by a decline in growth and activity of the organism. For convenience of reference, the total range of temperatures at which life is possible generally is divided into three "sub-ranges" into which are grouped those organisms whose optimum temperature falls within one of the sub-ranges. The three sub-ranges are cryophilic, mesophilic, and thermophilic. The boundary temperatures of each of the ranges have been somewhat arbitrarily assigned as being from about 5°C to about 10°C for the cryophilic range; from 10°C (or as high as 15°) to 40° or 45°C for the mesophilic range; and from 40° or 45°C to 70°C for the thermophilic range. (As is well known, certain blue-green algae and bacteria can survive and even grow at temperatures as high as 80 to 90°C.) Modern composting processes are designed to operate within the mesophilic and thermophilic ranges.

Much can be said in favor of composting at either of the two temperature ranges—mesophilic and thermophilic. The proponents of mesophilic composting (i.e., in the upper range—above 35°C) claim that mesophilic bacteria are more efficient than thermophilic bacteria, and that composting therefore proceeds more rapidly. An important advantage claimed by the proponents of thermophilic composting, in addition to improvement in the process, is that pathogens and weed seeds are killed at the high temperatures. This latter feature probably is one of the main reasons why most modern composting processes involve thermophilic composting at some stage in the overall process (3, 15, 16). Some evidence indicates that the process may proceed more efficiently in the lower thermophilic range, viz, 50° to 55°C (21, 40). All groups agree that the operating temperature should be at least 35°C.

The question of temperature probably is academic, since, as is explained in a later section of this chapter, the temperature of a reasonably large or insulated mass will gradually rise to well within the thermophilic range due to excess energy of microbial origin. This increase will inevitably take place unless positive measures are taken to dissipate the heat. Inasmuch as the heating involves no expenditure of external energy and positive measures would be needed to dissipate it, it would be more reasonable to design the operation to include thermophilic temperatures during the most active stages of the compost process.

There is no doubt that the process becomes less efficient when the temperature exceeds 60°C if for no other reason than that spore forming organisms begin to enter the spore or resistant stage at temperatures of 60°C and higher. When in the resistant or spore stage, activity diminishes to practically zero, and hence the composting process is correspondingly retarded.

The range of optimum temperatures for the composting process as a whole is quite broad, i.e., from about 35°C to about 55°C, because of the many groups of organisms taking part in the process. Each group has its particular optimum temperature which may or may not coincide with that of another group. Consequently, the optimum temperature for the process as a whole is an integration of, or perhaps better expressed, a compromise between the optimum temperatures of the various forms of microbes involved in the process. Of course, it should be remembered that unless a closely controlled digester is used, a uniform temperature does not prevail throughout the mass of composting material at any one time—except at the start of the process when all material is at ambient temperature. The existence of a plateau from the mesophilic into the thermophilic range is due not only to the involvement of many types of organisms, but also to adaptation of organisms to the temperature range.

At one time it had been thought that as far as bacterial activity was concerned, a kind of a "no-man's" land existed between the end of the mesophilic range and the beginning of the thermophilic range. The reason for the conviction was a supposedly sharp division of organisms into mesophiles and thermophiles. As for facultative organisms, it was thought that the alternative range was within either the strictly mesophilic or the strictly thermophilic ranges. However, studies by M. B. Allen (17) on the temperature requirements of aerobic sporeformers and by this author (18) on the effect of temperature on anaerobic digestion showed that the "no-man's" zone was an artifact arising from the conditions under which the temperatures were determined, —the prime source of error being the failure to use "adapted" or "acclimated" cultures.

At temperatures lower than 35°C, the efficiency and speed of the process increases with increase in temperature. The rate of increase begins to diminish as the temperature exceeds 30°C and approaches 35°C. The slope of a curve showing efficiency or speed of the process as a function of temperature would be practically a plateau between 35°C and about 55°C,—with perhaps some declination between 50°C and 55°C. As the temperature exceeds 55°C, efficiency and speed begin to drop abruptly and becomes negligible at temperatures in excess of 70°C. At temperatures above 65°C, sporeformers begin to lose their vegetative forms and assume spore forms. In the spore form, very little activity takes place. Nonsporeformers simply die off.

As stated earlier, in a practical operation, the desired temperature range includes thermophilic temperatures. The reasons are: 1) Some of the organisms involved in the process have their optimum temperature in the thermophilic range. 2) Weed seeds and most microbes of pathogenic significance cannot survive exposure to thermophilic temperatures. 3) Unless definite counter measures are taken, a composting mass of any appreciable volume will assume high temperatures.

Hydrogen Ion (pH) Level

Many of the reasons offered for the broad permissible temperature range apply to the factor pH level. As a generality one can state that the fungi tolerate a wider range of pH than do the bacteria. The optimum pH range for most bacteria is between 6 and 7.5, whereas for fungi it can be between 5.5 and 8.0. In fact, the upper pH limit for many fungi has been found to be a function of precipitation of essential nutrients from the growth medium, rather than of any inhibition due to pH *per se.*

In a practical operation, little can be done, or rather,

should be done to alter the pH level prevailing in the pile. The reasons are economics and nitrogen conservation. To change the pH requires the addition of a reagent, which in turn involves a twofold cost—that of the reagent and that of applying the reagent. Nitrogen conservation becomes a factor when taking steps to raise the pH level of the composting mass. The least expensive reagent for the purpose is lime. Unfortunately, the addition of lime usually is accompanied by an increase in ammonia formation and consequent loss of nitrogen (3, 19).

AVAILABILITY OF OXYGEN (AERATION)

Inasmuch as modern composting is almost universally aerobic, oxygen availability is an important environmental factor. In recent years, a study on the rate of oxygen uptake seems to be one of the first of the routine steps taken by a newcomer when he undertakes research concerned with composting. Among the earlier reports on oxygen uptake are those by Schulze (20, 21) and Popël (22). Schulze estimated that an air supply equivalent to 18,000 to 22,000 cu ft per ton of volatile matter per day was necessary in his studies to maintain aerobic conditions during peak oxygen demands. Chrometzka (23) names oxygen requirements ranging from 9mm^3/gram/hour for ripe compost to 284 mm^3/gram/hour for "fresh" compost (4 weeks old). "Fresh" refuse (7 days old) required 176 mm^3/gram/hour. He also reported that moisture content is a determinant of the oxygen requirement. For example, the requirement for fresh compost having a 45% moisture content was 263 mm^3/gram/hour; whereas with the moisture at 60%, it was 306 mm^3/gram/hour. Lossin (24) reports average chemical oxygen demands ranging from almost 900 mg/gram at one day to about 325 mg/gram at 24 days. Regan and Jeris (12) in a review of the decomposition of cellulose and refuse compiled a table listing oxygen uptake at various temperatures and moisture contents. The lowest uptake, 1.0 mg O_2/gram/ of volatile solids/hour took place when the temperature of the mass was 30°C and the moisture content was 45%. The highest uptake, 13.6 mg/gram

31

volatiles matter/hour, occurred when the temperature was 45°C and the moisture content was 56% (± 2%).

The variety of values cited in the preceding paragraph and in the table compiled by Regan and Jeris combine to emphasize two points, namely, the difficulty of determining true oxygen requirements and the desirability of using the chemical oxygen demand (COD) as a measurement of oxygen requirements. The difficulty of determining true or actual oxygen requirements in terms of rate, stems from the influence exerted by temperature, moisture content, size of bacterial population, and availability of nutrients on oxygen uptake. If one wishes to translate oxygen uptake into amount of aeration required to assure a supply of oxygen when it is needed, the problem becomes even more complex, because in addition to the preceding factors, the aeration equipment and physical nature and arrangement must be taken into consideration. The upshot of the preceding constraints is that while determining the absolute oxygen requirements of a composting mass is an interesting research undertaking, the findings are strictly limited in their application, namely to the material being tested and to the conditions of the test.

As a control measure in an ongoing operation, a monitoring of oxygen present in the exhaust air would be useful for mechanized composting. When the oxygen content of the exhaust drops below a few percent concentration, the rate of air input could be increased correspondingly. Monitoring could be done with the use of any reliable oxygen analyzing equipment. The monitoring of oxygen in a windrow type of operation would be on a far more crude level. In such a situation, the olfactory sense becomes the "instrument," and the basic principle is: The development of putrefactive odors indicates the onset of anaerobiosis, i.e., an insufficient oxygen supply.

GENETIC TRAITS

While not an environmental factor, genetic traits constitute the ultimate rate limiting factor. The significance of this statement is that regardless of how close to optimum all environmental conditions may be, the rate of decomposition depends upon the capability of microorganisms to break down the material. The capability of the microorganisms depends upon their genetic make-up; and the environment permits the expression of the genetic make-up.

A practical aspect of genetic limitations is that no amount of sophistication of equipment will hasten the decomposition of resistant materials beyond the limit permitted by the genetics of the organisms involved. It is this limitation that should prompt one to be skeptical of claims for one to three-day compost schemes, or of inoculums that will greatly accelerate decomposition beyond that normally encountered. Another practical aspect is that maintaining environmental conditions beyond the optimum level is a waste of effort, inasmuch as the potential as determined by the genetics of the organisms cannot be surpassed. On the other hand, there is no doubt that the process could be considerably accelerated over present-day rates by making a more effective provision for optimum conditions. However, the amount of gain would not necessarily warrant the extent of the required expenditures.

PART II.

The Process

The Process

Regardless of type, composting involves certain steps which in their order of sequence are as follows: sorting, grinding, composting, storage. Some systems call for another grinding after the composting step, and others call for screening as well as a second grinding.

Sorting

Since on the basis of present evidence, it appears that grinding of the raw material is one of the essential steps in aerobic composting, some degree of segregation of municipal refuse seems unavoidable. In cities using separate containers, the responsibility for segregating refuse might be imposed upon the individual householder by requiring that only specified organic material such as garbage, paper, *natural* rubber, leather, and rags be placed in the container intended for compostable material. It is difficult to believe however, that such an ordinance could be so strictly enforced as to preclude the occasional infraction which could result in severe damage or at least wear-and-tear to most of the several types of grinding mechanisms which might be used.

Materials which would normally require removal before grinding include tin cans, miscellaneous metals, glass, and ceramic ware. Excess paper might be removed for salvage, or in some cases to decrease the C/N ratio. Rags of natural fiber might be removed for salvage; whereas those of synthetic fiber should be removed because of their adverse effect on the appearance of the compost product.

Tin cans and other ferrous metal objects are commonly removed by a magnetic separator as the refuse moves along a conveyor belt. Rags and nonferrous objects are presently removed by hand. As time progresses and the necessary technology is developed, hand sorting will be replaced by mechanized sorting. Excess paper is removed by a blower with its suction intake located directly above the conveyor belt. Bottles and other glass and ceramic objects present one of the more difficult problems. Hand-picking is an unprofitable undertaking; and pulverizing glass mixed with garbage introduces difficult problems in equipment as well as excessive energy requirements. A project designed to compost municipal refuse must certainly envision the removal of metals, and until better equipment is available, the removal of glass as well.

Grinding

Grinding or shredding of refuse produces a number of beneficial results which hasten decomposition. The material is rendered more susceptible to bacterial invasion, made quite homogeneous, and given a beneficial aeration. It acquires a structure which facilitates handling and increases its response to moisture control and aeration. None of these characteristics is adversely affected by ground glass, but such material increases the already phenomenal abrasiveness of refuse, which is capable of destroying the cutting edges of hammermill and similar blades in a single day's operation. Unless the glass is pulverized, shards left in the material detract from the quality of the compost product.

The aim of grinding is to chop refuse into small pieces. There are no special size requirements, but the material must not be pulped lest it become too soggy to compost. The ideal particle size would be the minimum size at which undue compaction would not occur. The larger the particle size, the slower will be the rate of decomposition. For municipal refuse, a particle size within the range of 1 to 2 inches would be suitable.

Composting

DESCRIPTION

This is the step in which the procedures for windrow and mechanized composting differ. A detailed description of the technology involved in this step is reserved for a separate section in this chapter. At this point, the concern is with what happens to the composting material.

Immediately after the material has been ground and either has been stacked in windrows or placed in a digester, bacterial activity begins to proceed at an accelerated pace. The first easily recognized manifestation of this activity is an increase in the temperature of the mass—provided the volume is large enough to accomplish self insulation, or the heat is not dissipated by blowing, etc. The temperature rises at a rate determined by the environmental factors and the nature of the material. In the University of California studies (3), the temperature generally increased from ambient to 50°C within one or two days after the material had been stacked in windrows. After four days, the temperature was between 60° and 70°C. The highest temperature reached in a pile was 75°C. The shape of the temperature curve shown in Figure 1 is typical for "high-rate" windrow composting of municipal refuse. The time scale will differ according to the way in which the material is handled. In an undisturbed pile, the high temperatures prevail from the center of the mass to the outer 2 to 4-inch layer.

The temperature rise is noticeable even in mechanized composting, because the digesters are constructed such that heat does not readily escape, and the composting material is present in large enough masses to bring about some self insulation. However, the distribution of temperature level is more uniform throughout the mass.

The high degree of bacterial activity is indicated by the fact that the temperature drop accompanying the turning operation in windrow composting is very minor, and the temperature is regained within a very short time after turning is completed. As stated earlier, the heat is due to the excess energy released by the bacteria. Inasmuch as the heat energy does not escape from the composting material at a rate faster than it is generated, the temperature of the mass begins to rise. The high temperature is maintained until the readily decomposable material has been broken down. As that point is approached, bacterial activity begins to decline, and the temperature drops correspondingly.

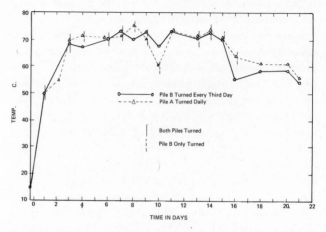

FIGURE 1. Temperature Curve Typical of "High-Rate" Windrow Compost Pile (3)

The physical appearance of the material undergoes a change during the process. Municipal refuse has a greyish-green color after being ground. This color gradually turns to brown or brownish-gray, and the transition generally is completed within four or five days after grinding. Corrugated cardboard, unprinted paper, and other organic items lose their identity, whereas printed newsprint is recognizable throughout the process. As the home gardener is aware, composted manures look much like dehydrated fresh manure. Bedding material in the manure retains its identity, but becomes quite brittle and fragile. Cannery waste loses its characteristic appearance and assumes the dark color associated with compost.

A noteworthy change is that of the odor of the composting material. Ground municipal refuse has a somewhat pungent odor. If the University of California method of windrow composting is followed, the material loses its pungent odor and assumes the earthy odor of a rich soil within six or seven days after the material has been ground and windrowed. A similar pattern takes place when manures or cannery wastes are composted, in that both lose their characteristic odors and assume the earthy odor.

Other characteristic changes that take place are an increase in oxygen uptake, a shift in the redox potential, a rise in pH level, the development of olfactorily detectable ammonia, and a drop in the C/N ratio. The oxygen uptake has been discussed in a previous section. The shift in redox potential is that which characteristically takes place when conditions change from anaerobic to aerobic. Typically, the pH level drops during the first few days of composting due to the synthesis of organic acid by the bacteria. If the composting material has anaerobic zones, some butyric acid, acetic, and propionic acid may be formed. However, the acids are soon utilized as substrate by the bacteria; and with the formation of ammonia, the pH level of the pile begins to rise. The lowest pH levels observed in the University studies were on the order of 5.0 to 6.0; and the highest, from 8.5 to 9.5. The discussion on ammonia production in the section on the C/N ratio fairly well covered the pertinent points of that phenomenon. The drop in C/N ratio during the compost step is due to the release of CO_2 into the ambient air. The CO_2 is that formed by bacteria when oxidizing the carbonaceous material in the pile. Very little, if any, nitrogen fixation takes place.

DETERMINATION OF DEGREE OF STABILIZATION

The net result of the composting step is the stabilization of the organic matter in the wastes. The extent of stabilization is relative, in that the material is not completely stabilized, i.e., rendered inert. Ultimate stabilization of organic matter would result in the end products CO_2, H_2O, and mineral ash. Obviously, this does not occur in conventional composting, nor is it to be desired either in terms of utility of the product or of practicality of attainment. The impracticality arises from the excessive time factor involved. The utility of the compost product, as will be explained later, depends upon its further breakdown in the soil.

The desired degree of stability is one at which the material will not give rise to nuisances when stored—even if it should be wetted. The problem in a compost operation

41

is one of determining when this point is reached. It is important in a practical operation, because unnecessary handling can be avoided through removal of the material from the plant directly the proper degree of stabilization is attained. Of less immediate import, but nevertheless essential, is that an accurate and uniform procedure of stability determination makes it possible to evaluate the various compost systems on the market. Thus, how can one weigh the claims of the entrepreneur for his machine which according to him, composts refuse in 6 days against that of another and more modest one, who claims 12 days for his machine? The one may term a material composted when it has assumed a dark color; while the more modest one relies on final temperature drop as the indicator of stability.

Finding a solution to the problem has challenged several researchers. Change in appearance is not a criterion. The University of California studies showed that the dark color typical of composted material may be attained long before the necessary degree of stability is reached. The same may be said about the development of the earthy odor. The earthy odor is characteristic of actinomycetes, consequently the earthy odor would be expected when those organisms are active. Since the actinomycetes require a decomposable substrate, their presence, at least at their first manifestation, would indicate the existence of "unstable" organic matter.

Parameters of stability other than appearance and odor, are final drop in temperature (3), degree of self-heating capacity (25), amount of decomposable and resistant organic matter in the material (26), rise in redox potential (27), oxygen uptake (23), growth of *Chaetomium gracile* (28), and the starch test (29).

As mentioned earlier, in the University studies, it was observed that the attainment of a satisfactory degree of stabilization was always accompanied by a final and inevitable decline in temperature. The finality of the decline was confirmed by failure of the temperature to rise despite the imposition of favorable environmental conditions. It also was observed that once the temperature had receded to about 45°C to 50°C, the material had become sufficiently stabilized to permit indefinite storage. Therefore, as far as windrow composting is concerned, the final drop in temperature is an excellent measure of stability.

Niese's (25) self-heating capability analysis is a variation of the "final drop in temperature" parameter. With Niese's method, a sample of the material is placed in Dewar flasks. The containers are covered with several layers of cotton wadding held together with cellulose tape. Temperatures are measured by way of a suitable sensing device. The flasks are placed in an incubator in which the temperature is regulated by a temperature-difference device to eliminate heat loss from the flasks. The height of the temperature reached in the flasks indicates the extent of stability of the material. For example, results obtained by Niese indicate a temperature above 70°C for raw refuse, 40 to 60°C for "medium" decomposition, and under 30°C for "complete" stabilization.

The principle underlying Rolle and Orsonic's method of determining decomposable and resistant organic matter (26) is the ascertaining of the amount of oxidizing reagent used in the test. It consists in treating the sample with a potassium dichromate solution in the presence of sulfuric acid. A certain amount of dichromate added in excess is thereby used up in the eradication of organic matter. The oxidizing agent left at the end of the reaction is back-titrated with ferrous ammonium sulfate, and the amount of potassium dichromate used up is established. The amount of decomposable organic matter is calculated as follows:

$$ DOM = m^l \, N \left(1 - \frac{T}{S} \cdot 1.34 \right) $$

in which DOM is decomposable organic matter, m^l is m^l of $K_2Cr_2O_7$ solution; N is normality of the $K_2Cr_2O_7$. Quantitatively, resistant organic matter is that amount of loss by combustion that is not degraded in the oxidation reaction.

The oxidation-reaction potential determination of stability (27) is based on the fact that the presence of decomposable organic substances leads to an intensification of microbial conversion, which in turn brings about increase in oxygen uptake and accompanying drop in oxidation-reduction potential. Möller (37) states that the material in a pile of compost may be regarded as sufficiently stabilized when the redox potential of the core of the pile is <50 mV below that of the outer layer.

The *Chaetomium* method as described by Obrist (28) is based on the measurement of growth and formation of fruiting bodies of the fungus *Chaetomium gracilis* cultured on a solid nutrient medium containing pulverized refuse or compost. After an incubation period of 12 days, the fruiting bodies are counted. Growth and number of fruiting bodies are functions of the amount of decomposable material present in the tested material.

The starch determination method as developed by Lossin (29) depends on the assumption that the more advanced the degree of decomposition, the less the amount of decomposable organic matter. He states that three types of carbohydrates are found in composting material, namely, sugars, starch, and cellulose. In windrow composting, sugars disappear within a week after the start of the process. Starch passes through its maximum degradation in the fourth to fifth week of composting.

A characteristic of all of the preceding tests, excepting perhaps the two depending upon temperature level or drop, is that they are relative, in that the determination rests on a change in values, rather than on a standard, consistent number. Hence, they cannot be used as standards for wide scale application. The measurement of the redox potential is still not sufficiently accurate and is subject to a variety of interfering factors. The measuring procedure for self-heating is a slow one and may require several days to complete. The *Chaetomium* test is time-consuming, and is dependent to a large extent on the skill of the tester. The success of the starch rests on the universal presence of starch in refuse and compost. That starch always is present in refuse remains to be demonstrated.

DURATION OF COMPOSTING STAGE

As indicated earlier, the required duration of the composting step is a function of procedure and environmental conditions. In the University studies times ranged from 10 to 11 days for composting garden residue to about 21 days for a refuse having a high C/N ratio (78:1). Some purveyors of compost equipment name times as short as 3 to 6 days with their systems. However, if one carefully studies their claims, he will find that the complete directions call for a 2- to 6-week "maturation" period after the "active" composting has been completed in the digester. In reality, the material prior to "maturing" is far from being ready for use or for storage. Anyone not thoroughly conversant with composting should be highly skeptical of exaggerated claims of high-speed composting.

In a practical operation, speed of the process is not usually a critical factor in terms of economics, since the market is such that the material must be stored. It becomes important if the type of equipment used is expensive to operate. In such a situation, the less the exposure time in the composter, the more that can be processed per day, and the cost per ton will be that much lower. The answer to the latter problem is to invest in a less expensive composter, even if the required time for composting is thereby lengthened by a few days.

VOLUME REDUCTION

The extent of volume reduction is a function of nature of the waste and the duration of the compost time. The degree of reduction increases in proportion to the amount of readily decomposable material in the wastes. In the University studies, the reduction in volume with garden debris was as much as 60 to 65%. On the other hand, when municipal refuse having a heavy concentration of newsprint was composted, the reduction in volume was from 30 to 35%.

Final Processing and Storage

FINAL PROCESSING

After the material is adjudged sufficiently stable to store, it is ready for "rough" applications, i.e., in large scale agriculture, land reclamation, etc.

In practice, the usual procedure is to sort the compost into fractions on the basis of quality. This is usually done by screening the material. The coarsest material is destined for the "rough" applications, while the finest is reserved for the home gardener for "luxury" crops. Often the material remaining after the separation of the coarser fraction is ground and screened. Grinding compost is less a chore than grinding raw refuse due to the fact that the material has been rendered more amenable to grinding because of having been composted. Of course, the major benefit of the second grinding is the increase in "eye" appeal which results.

As stated earlier, properly composted material can be stored without danger of subsequent generation of nuisances. Although decomposition will occur during storage unless the moisture content is too low for bacterial activity, the rate of decomposition will be very slow, and no odorous intermediates are formed.

PART III.

Technology

Technology

Development

It has become almost a cliché to begin a historical sketch of composting with the statement that it ranks with the oldest of the agricultural activities of man. However, taken in the strict sense of the definition, the development of a truly systematic approach to composting began with Sir Albert Howard's work in Indore, India in the early 1930's (30), in which he systemized the traditional procedure in collaboration with Jackson and Wad. His process became known as the Indore process because of the locale of his activities. The Indore process involves piling on open ground to a height of about five feet, or placing in pits, alternate layers of readily putrescible materials such as garbage, night soil, animal manure, or sewage sludge, and relatively stable organic matter such as straw and leaves. The mass is usually turned twice during the composting process.

While Sir Albert was refining practices that had been in use in India and China, others, especially in Europe, were directing considerable effort towards mechanizing the composting process. A variety of mechanical devices were designed and patented during the decade 1920 to 1930. Some of the devices were intended to improve the aesthetics of the process by enclosing it, while others were developed hopefully to speed the process.

Among the early mechanized processes, was one developed by G. Giovanni Beccari of Florence, Italy (34, 35, 36). The Beccari process combines an initial anaerobic fermentation stage and a final aerobic stage. The anaerobic fermentation takes place in an enclosed cell designed to prevent the escape of foul odors usually associated with the initial breakdown of putrescible material under anaerobic conditions. As time goes by, vents are opened to admit air, and thereby to permit further decomposition to take place under partially aerobic conditions. The amount of aerobic decomposition under such conditions would be limited to the upper inch or two of the surface layer, and therefore the greater part of the mass continues in an anaerobic state, unless it is stirred or disturbed in some manner. As originally designed, the Beccari cell consisted of a simple suboidal cell with a loading hatch on the top and an unloading door on the front. Valves or other closures were incorporated in the structure as air vents. The process was later modified to provide for recirculation of gases or of drainage liquors. The modified process became known as the Verdier process.

In 1931, Jean Bordas (37) further modified the Beccari process. He attempted to eliminate the anaerobic stage by introducing forced air into a fermentation silo. His attempt was the first to be aimed at eliminating or minimizing the anaerobic phase. Bordas' silo was divided by a grate into an upper and lower section, and air was introduced along the walls and through a central pipe. With the Bordas' silo, compost is produced by a batch process, maximum usage of the silo being accomplished by dropping the charge through the grate into the lower chamber after it has lost appreciable volume through decomposition.

The concept of aeration was carried a step further by the development of a multiple grate digester to produce compost by a continuous aerobic process. The process was patented in 1939 by Earp-Thomas. In the Earp-Thomas silo, aeration is accomplished by a combination of rotating plows and forced air. A feature, insisted by Earp-Thomas as being essential, was the use of special cultures of bacteria furnished by Earp-Thomas.

A later variation of the digester type of enclosed cell was designed by Ralph W. Riker Company of Lansing, Michigan. It consisted of a double walled silo with multiple floors. The inner silo was aerated internally and externally, and the decomposing mass was sprayed continuously with drainage liquor pumped from a collecting sump positioned in the base of the silo.

A different approach to digester design is represented

by the one patented by Frazer in 1949 (38). The Frazer process is a fully mechanized and continuous one, in which compost is supposedly produced rapidly and under aerobic conditions. Organic matter is shredded and introduced into a machine where it is kept continuously agitated as it moves from one level to another and is brought into contact with the gases of decomposition—a salient feature of the patent. The scientific naiveté shown in the patent language is illustrated by the provision for recirculating "activated" carbon dioxide through the composting mass. The finished product passes through and out the bottom through a screen. Tailings from the screen are recycled.

The Dano process marks a step in the direction of a more sound approach to the design of equipment for composting. As originally designed, the Dano process was essentially a separating and grinding process. Later developments in the process involved the use of a slowly rotating horizontal drum suitably equipped for injecting air, applying moisture, and controlling temperature.

Present Technology

WINDROW SYSTEMS

Types of windrow systems range from the rather primitive one designed by Sir Albert Howard to the relatively advanced one developed at the University of California in the 1950's. As explained in the section on Classification, windrow or open composting systems are characterized by having the composting take place in the open by placing the ground refuse in elongated piles, i.e., windrows. Aeration is accomplished by periodically turning the piles in a manner such that all particles are exposed to comparable conditions at some time during the course of the active period of the compost process.

Excepting in the northern tier of states in the U.S., the pile may be on any open, surface-drained area, although a shed roof might be advisable over that portion of the piles still in the active composting stage. In colder climates, it would be advisable to more completely protect the active portion of the piles by providing sides to the shed. Of course, in all cases, the separation, grinding, and other mechanical components should be completely protected. Windrows may be of any convenient length, but the depth of the pile is somewhat critical. If piled too high, the material will be compressed by its own weight, pore space is lost, and the mass becomes anaerobic. In some instances, the maximum practical height may be governed by the equipment used for stacking the ground refuse, or by the tendency of the pile to get excessively hot—above 70°C. A pile that is too shallow loses heat too rapidly, and optimum temperatures for thermophilic organisms are not attained. In addition, loss of moisture is excessive, especially near the edges of the pile and the rate of composting is thereby retarded.

Although experience quickly demonstrates the most suitable height of pile for any particular refuse, a maximum of 5 or 6 feet is recommended for freshly ground municipal refuse. As the material loses volume during decomposition, any desired height of pile can be maintained by reducing or expanding the width of the windrow at the time it is turned.

The initial width of a windrow probably will not exceed 8 or 10 feet at the base for convenience in turning. In dry weather, the cross section is usually made trapezoidal, with the top width governed by the width of the base and the angle of repose of the material, which is something like 30 degrees from the vertical. In rainy climates or in wet weather, the cross section of the windrow should be approximately semi-circular like a haycock in order to shed water. In that case, the maximum permissible height of pile will govern its maximum width.

Other than maximum and minimum heights of pile, there is nothing critical about the stacking of ground refuse for composting; hence in each individual case, experience with the materials handling equipment employed will establish the best practice to be followed.

Turning. Since aeration in windrow composting is accomplished by turning, the pile is turned fairly frequently so as to obtain the rapid, nuisance free decomposition characteristic of the thermophilic aerobic process. Uniform decomposition essential to rapid composting is insured by turning the outer edges into the center of the pile at each turn. In this manner, any fly larvae, pathogens, or insect eggs which might survive at the cooler surface are exposed to the lethal temperatures of the interior of the pile. This means that neither a simple overturn nor a vertical expansion of the pile constitutes adequate turning. An inward mixing of material from both sides of the pile is required.

Secondary reasons for a particular turning operation might be reduction of the initial moisture content, and reclamation of a compost pile which has become anaerobic. Anaerobic conditions usually result from too great a moisture content for the normal turning schedule practiced. Excess moisture may be inherent in the particular refuse being composted, or it may result from continual soaking by rain, especially during periods of turning, when composting is done in the open. Anaerobic conditions may also occur as the result of equipment breakdown, a long period of unusually bad weather, or other interruption of a normal turning schedule.

The frequency of turning and the total number of turns required during the composting process are governed largely by the moisture content. Experience gained during the University studies indicates that for municipal refuse the following turning schedule is adequate: If the initial moisture is less than 70%, the first turn should be made on the third day. Thereafter turn as follows until the 11th or 12th day:

Moisture 60 to 70%: Turn at 2-day intervals. Number of required turns—about 5.

Moisture 40 to 60%: Turn at 3-day intervals. Approximate number of turns—4.

Moisture below 40%: Add moisture.

If the moisture is more than 70%, turn everyday until the moisture content is reduced to less than 70%, then follow the above schedule.

In following the schedule of turning, it is not necessary to determine moisture content after the initial analysis. Experience soon enables the operator to estimate the need for adding moisture and the adequacy of a turning schedule. A good rule of thumb is to begin a schedule of daily turning at the onset of any foul odors that are noticed when a pile is disturbed either by turning or by digging into it for inspection purposes. Daily turning should be continued thereafter until the odor disappears. No matter how anaerobic a pile may become, it will recover under a schedule of daily turning, which reduces the moisture and provides aeration.

Inasmuch as turning of municipal refuse normally should be done at intervals of 2 or 3 days, any partially anaerobic conditions quickly disappear. Turning can be omitted on week ends, so that this step does not involve extraordinary costs.

Turning has sometimes been advocated as a means of dissipating the heat of a compost pile in which the temperature exceeds 75°C. In the University studies, however, the temperature drop upon turning was only 5 to 10 degrees, which was recovered within 2 or 3 hours. In any event, a shallower pile would control the maximum temperature without the labor involved in turning.

The turning program outlined in the preceding paragraphs is geared to "high-speed" composting. Where time is not an important constraint, the turning schedule can be modified to allow longer intervals between turning. The same directive applies when nitrogen conservation is an important consideration, because turning accelerates nitrogen loss.

Bottom Aeration. Various substitutes have been proposed for turning as an aeration method. Among these are placing the ground refuse in wire containers (39, 40), stacking the material on slotted or perforated floors, and forcing air into the pile by way of bottom aeration. Placing the material in wire bins only succeeds in aerating the outer layers of the mass. Practically the same exposure is obtained by stacking the material. Resorting to slotted or perforated floors allows a little additional exposure to air, but not enough to warrant the expense and inconvenience involved in providing this exposure.

While the concept of forced aeration may be a sound one in many applications, many difficulties combine to diminish its utility in the windrow composting of municipal refuse. Probably, the major difficulty is that of diffusing the air throughout the pile so that all parts of the pile are uniformly aerated. In a practical application involving municipal refuse, channels form in the pile and the forced air then short-circuits through these channels. Moreover, because of the evaporation brought about by the passage of air, the material in the immediate vicinity of the channels becomes excessively dry. Even were forced aeration successful in its purpose, the piles would have to be turned occasionally so as to bring about the necessary exposure of all particles to the high interior temperatures and to insure uniform decomposition.

Moisture Control. The control of moisture in windrow composting may range from eliminating excess moisture to applying water when a pile becomes too dry.

As stated earlier, a number of additives may be used with varying degrees of effectiveness to control excessive moisture. If excess paper is being segregated, some degree of control may be obtained by leaving a part of the paper in the refuse. Because paper is of limited effectiveness however, there is danger of using too much and thereby producing an excessively high C/N ratio. While straw may be effective in controlling moisture and has the added advantage of improving the structure of the material, the increased cost involved in buying and handling it as well as the uncertainty of its availability at some seasons of the year, make its use impractical in ordinary composting. Dry soil or sawdust are other additives effective in lowering moisture content. Here again, the problem of availability and cost of handling limit their use. Whenever any additive is used, care must be taken to add it in amounts which will not unduly increase the C/N ratio. The recommended remedy for excessive moisture is frequent turning. This brings about a reduction in moisture content without disturbing the C/N ratio.

The foregoing considerations concern high initial moisture. In areas where rainfall is heavy, material being composted in the open may become excessively wet. Therefore, preventive measures should be taken. If economic conditions make impossible the obvious remedy, namely sheltering the piles with a roof, then the tops of the piles or windrows can be rounded, so that the outer surface will shed water much as does a thatched roof. Wiley of Dumfriesshire in Scotland (41) has reported that material stacked in this manner will withstand intermittent heavy rainfall, but continuous rainfall will soak the pile. Van Vuren (7) likewise reports soaking of composting material subjected to repeated rainfalls without sufficient dry intervals. In the University studies, the composting material was subjected to one heavy rainfall. The rain penetrated only one-eighth to one-quarter of an inch. Attempts to add moisture by sprinkling with a hose produced similar results. The water merely flowed off the piles without penetrating them. If piles should become waterlogged, turning will remedy the situation. Of course, no turning should be done during a rainfall, because all parts of the open stack will be exposed to rain and an increase in moisture content will result.

To bring up the moisture content of a pile, water can be added most effectively during the turning operation, at which time the exposed material absorbs water. The outer parts of unsheltered piles have a tendency to dry out during sunny weather, in which case surface sprinkling should be practiced to promote uniform decomposition.

Design Considerations: An experienced designer can readily develop a plant layout for receiving, segregating, and grinding refuse, and for stacking, turning, regrinding, and stockpiling or storing finished compost. The first three of these operations would presumably be done under cover. The cheapest industrial type of building should suffice.

In determining the necessary land area the length of compost piles may be taken as multiples of one day's production, with interruption in continuity, perhaps, to give flexibility to the turning schedule. Spacing of piles may be determined from the proposed turning procedures and the maneuvering space required for the stacking and turning equipment. These considerations together with the period of composting anticipated would determine the land area necessary for any particular composting operation. At least 100% excess land should be available for contingencies such as inability to finish compost on schedule because of breakdown of equipment or excess rain. The land area might be as little as 8 or 10 acres for a population of 100,-000, although more would perhaps be advisable.

Costs: The literature is fairly sparse with respect to references to the economics of windrow composting, probably because most attention in the U.S. has been directed towards mechanical composting. One analysis made in recent years is that by Hart et al (47) for the type of composting required for their "garbage farming" system. Inasmuch as Hart's system involves a minimum of composting, the major costs are those of grinding and land-use charges. He estimates grinding costs as being on the order of $3.00 per ton (includes all costs pertinent to grinding); and land charges to be about $4.60 per ton, if land costs are $4,000 per acre and interest is 6%, and the land is loaded at 400 tons of compost per acre.

An estimate made so long ago (i.e. in 1958 [43]) as to have mainly a historical value makes the following breakdown: The plant would have a 265-ton per day capacity, and would be operated 8 hours per day, 5 days per week. The plant would produce 125 tons of compost and 80 tons of marketable scrap per day. The required capital investment would be $715,000. Labor costs would be $2.45 per ton; and other costs, $0.45 per ton. Nothing was said about grinding costs. In a 1961 survey of European compost practice, Wiley (44) quotes a capital cost of $5,330 per ton rate capacity and $4.54 per ton of refuse for operating and amortizing costs.

The most recent (1971) cost estimates of windrow composting are to be found in a report issued by the U.S. Environmental Protection Agency (45) on the Johnson City demonstration compost studies. The estimates are based on actual costs encountered at the Johnson City plant. Capital costs (in 1969-dollars) range from $16,560 per ton of daily capacity for a 50-ton per day plant to $5,460 per ton of daily capacity for a 200-ton per day plant on a 2-shift operation. The estimates of the total yearly capital investments for the plants as based on cost per ton of refuse processed would be $6.12 per ton for the 50-ton per day plant and $2.10 per ton for the 200-ton per day plant. Estimated operating costs range from $13.65 per ton for the 50-ton per day plant to $8.70 per ton for the 200-ton per day 2-shift plant. These values probably are higher than those that would prevail were a less elaborate plant used.

Mechanized Systems: The design of most of the mechanical composters is based on providing aeration by some type of tumbling or stirring action. Thus, some digesters are equipped with moving plows to stir the material. A horizontal digester has vanes to carry the composting material to a point at which it drops or tumbles to the bottom of the cylinder and again is carried up. Other types provide the tumbling by having the material drop from one floor to the next in a multi-storied digester. A successful system (Metrowaste) combines bottom aeration and aeration by tumbling accomplished by passing a mobile endless belt from one end of the compost chamber (bin) to the other. As the belt moves, it picks up compost at its front, lifts it to a height of about 3 feet and allows the material to drop behind it. Another method (Fairfield-Hardy) combines stirring with forced aeration by having large hollow augurs rotating through the composting mass. The augurs have nozzles out of which air is forced into the material as the augurs are rotated.

In addition to providing aeration, mechanical digesters are equipped to ensure adequate temperature and moisture control.

Land Requirements: The land requirements for a mechanical digester operation are on the order of 2.5 to 3 acres for a 100-ton per day plant. This number allows for about a 6-month's stockpile to cover periods when the demand for the product is low.

Costs: The literature is more profuse in economic analyses of mechanized composting than for windrow composting. A report on European installations in 1966 (46) states an average cost of $4.55 to process one ton of refuse. Of this amount, 1.76 was for all capital costs. In an article, Harding (47) gives estimates of costs (1968) for three different composting systems. His estimates are repeated herein for only two of the systems, because no example of the third system presently is in operation in the U.S. He quotes a capital cost for a Fairfield digester (exclusive of land and land improvement costs) ranging from $1.4 million dollars for a 100-ton per day plant to $1.6 million for a 400-ton per day plant. Respective energy requirements are 900 and 2,500 HP; and manpower requirements, 8 and 20. Capital costs for a Metrowaste plant range from $900,000 for a 100-ton per day plant to $1.6 million for a 400-ton per day plant. Respective energy requirements are 1,250 HP and 2,000 HP. Labor needs are 12 and 30 men respectively. The authors of the Johnson City compost report (45) estimate the investment cost per ton daily capacity (exclusive of land) to be $2,005. Land costs ($4,000 per acre) would add $18 per ton of capacity. The total investment costs per ton of refuse processed would add up to $0.75. The authors state that the estimated operating cost of the mechanized plant at Gainesville, Florida, ranged from $7.56 on a 157-ton per day basis to $6.94 per ton on a 346-ton per day basis.

Special Application

Composting has an attractive potential in the disposal of animal and cannery wastes. These two types of wastes pose major problems in disposal, which will be aggravated as the rate of production of these wastes increases. Their physical characteristics are such that they readily give rise to nuisances in the form of objectionable odors and attraction of flies. Both types are characterized by a moisture content high enough to make incineration an expensive operation. Burying the material in a sanitary landfill not only is a noisome operation but also increases the danger of pollution of ground and surface waters.

Because of their highly putrescible nature, animal and cannery wastes are especially amenable to composting. The main drawback is their high moisture content. The problem is more severe with cannery wastes because their moisture content generally far surpasses that of animal wastes. Space does not permit a description and evaluation of the various methods that have been proposed to solve the problem, and hence only two are treated herein.

One of the methods is for the treatment of dairy manures containing no bedding materials. The system was developed by Senn of the University of California at Los Angeles School of Public Health as a part of a project aimed at developing ways of disposing of dairy wastes. In essence, the process entails air-drying the manure until its moisture content drops to 60% or less. In an on-going process, the drying step needs be done only once—i.e., at the initiation of a given operation. The dried material is mixed with fresh material in a proportion such that the mixture does not "cake," and is placed in a bin. The bin is equipped for forced bottom aeration. No problem is encountered in aerating the material in this manner, provided the moisture content is not excessive. By the time the material is composted, its moisture content is low enough to permit it to serve as a moisture absorbent for fresh manure. A variation is to spread the composted material in the cows' stalls to serve as a bedding for the animals and to absorb moisture from fresh manure. This system is applicable to any animal waste.

A system for the continuous composting of cannery wastes was developed by the National Canners Association Research Laboratory (19) which can be successfully used in composting cannery wastes. With the system, the wastes can be composted either in windrows or in bins. The distinguishing feature of the system is that the composted product is used repeatedly as a moisture absorbent for the incoming wastes. The moisture content of the initial charge is lowered by adding sawdust, rice hulls, or other dry absorbent materials. Once the process has begun, the need for importing outside materials for absorption ceases to exist.

PART IV.

Health Aspects

Health Aspects

Historical

The early concern with the public health aspects of composting stemmed from the fact that in European practice night soil was a common component of material to be composted. The concern was over the survival of pathogens and parasites from the night soil. The major effort in research on public health aspects of composting continues to be centered in Europe.

An apparent absence of health hazards was a characteristic common to all well managed composting operations in the Old World. Thus, in the early 1950's, the Medical Research Council in England was able to find no risk from the manufacture of compost. Van Vuren (7) could not demonstrate any dangers in properly managed composting operations in South Africa. Van Vuren's findings were corroborated in the results of studies made by Blair (48) and others in South Africa. The Agricultural Research Council in England (49) noted also that fly larvae were sharply curtailed in the compost operations. A similar observation was made by Van Vuren.

In the 1950's, no similar record of experience was available in the U.S. The University of California researchers (3) observed that while the refuse coming into the process had a heavy concentration of fly larvae, by the time the material had been passed through the grinder, all larvae were destroyed. No fly activity was noted in the composting material. In studies on composting of farm and garden wastes (50), no evidence of fly development could be found either in composting manures or garden wastes. Although the University researchers made no attempt to isolate pathogens and parasites from their compost piles, they did compile a table showing the thermal death points of some common pathogens and parasites (3), and reasoned from the information in the table that disease causing organisms would not survive in a well-managed compost operation (50). Table II is a reproduction of the table. Unfortunately, this table was offered by many writers in the following years as sole evidence of the safety of composting without having recourse to actual experimentation.

TABLE II.

THERMAL DEATH POINTS OF SOME COMMON PATHOGENS AND PARASITES

Organism

Salmonella typhosa: No growth beyond 46°C; death within 30 min. at 55° to 60°C.
Salmonella spp.: Death within one hour at 56°C; death within 15 to 20 min. at 60°C.
Shigella spp.: Death within one hour at 55°C.
Escherichia coli: Most die within one hour at 55°C; and within 15 to 20 min. at 60°C.
Endamoeba histolytica: Thermal death point is 68°C.
Taenia saginata: Death within 5 min. at 71°C.
Trichinella spiralis larvae: ineffectivity reduces as a result of one hour exposure at 50°C; thermal death point is 62 to 72°C.
Necator americanus: Death within 50 min. at 45°C.
Brucella abortus or *suis*: Death within three minutes at 61°C.
Micrococcus pyogenes var. *aureus*: Death within 10 min. at 50°C.
Streptococcus pyogenes: Death within 10 min. at 54° C.
Mycobacterium tuberculosis: var. *hominis*: Death within 15 to 20 min. at 66°C; or monetary heating at 67°C.
Mycobacterium diptheriae: Death within 45 min. at 55°C.

Studies of a more scientific or definitive nature were made in 1959 and in the 1960's in Europe by Strauch (8), Banse (51), Farkasdi (51), and Knoll (52). Their concern is the fate of pathogens that might be introduced with sewage sludge in an operation involving the composting of sludge and refuse. Knoll (52) studied the survival of strains of

66

Salmonella (*typhimurium, cairo, infantis,* and *typhi*). Under the conditions prevailing in the experimental compost set-up, no organisms survived over a span of 14 days. Banse *et al* used *Salmonella* and *Bacillus anthracis* as the test organisms in their studies. They found that *Salmonella* was rendered harmless within 3 to 5 days, whereas *B. anthracis* survived over a period of 7 days. Results of studies made during the compost studies at Johnson City, Tennessee showed that properly managed windrow composting turns out a product that is safe for agricultural and garden use (53, 54). The test organism in the studies was *M. tuberculosis*.

Unfortunately, at the time this chapter was written no work on viruses had been reported in the literature available to this author.

Principles

The major factors in the destruction of pathogenic organisms in the compost process are heat and antibiotic reactions. As pointed out earlier, temperatures in the upper 60's (Centigrade) and lower 70's are normally reached during the course of the process. These temperatures exceed the thermal death point of the organisms listed in Table II. Not only are the high temperatures reached, they persist for a matter of days, i.e., in excess of the time required to kill the organisms.

As Knoll (52) demonstrated, the extermination of pathogens is not solely a thermal reaction. Antibiotic phenomena play an important part. In Knoll's experiments the test organisms survived much longer when exposed only to high temperatures in the composting material than when they were placed in contact with other organisms. One would expect the synthesis of antibiotic substances to occur, in view of the wide array of microorganisms, especially of actinomycetes and fungi. Of course, competition for nutrient must also have a part in the destruction. However, the effects of competition for nutrient would probably be more inhibitory than lethal.

The adverse effects on flies in their various stages of development are both thermal and nutritional in origin. The higher temperatures are considerably in excess of the thermal death point of the fly in all of its stages of development. Chemical and physical changes in the nature of the materials being composted soon render them unfit as a nutrient source for flies. Consequently, while adult flies may alight on a pile, they rarely remain long enough to deposit eggs.

In concluding this section on public health, it is emphasized that the beneficial effects of composting can be realized only by careful control of all phases of the process. Care must be taken that all particles are exposed to high temperatures and that all particles receive full exposure to the process. In view of the well nigh impossibility of maintaining perfect control at all times, the composting of night-soil or of raw sewage sludge with refuse should be undertaken with great reluctance. The resulting compost product should be subjected to heat sterilization. If not sterilized, its use should be restricted to applications that involve no human contact, directly or indirectly.

PART V.

Use of the Product

Use of the Product

Nature and Value of Finished Compost

VALUE AS A SOIL CONDITIONER

Finished compost may be designated by the general term "humus." When used in the soil, humus has many characteristics beneficial both to the soil itself and to growing vegetation. In conjunction with commercial fertilizers, humus exhibits certain additional and very desirable characteristics. Organic acids resulting from the metabolic breakdown of organic material form a complex with the inorganic phosphate. In this form, phosphorus is more readily available to higher plants. Both phosphorus and nitrogen are involved in a storing effect peculiar to humus. The precipitation of phosphorus by calcium is inhibited; and nitrogen by being converted into bacterial protoplasm is rendered insoluble. Thereafter, the nitrogen becomes available as the bacteria die and decompose. The effect is to prevent leaching of soluble inorganic nitrogen and to make its rate of availability more nearly equal to that at which plants can utilize it. The gradual decomposition of insoluble organic matter by microorganisms results in a continual liberation of nitrogen as ammonia, which is then oxidized to nitrites and nitrates.

The physical effects of humus on the soil are perhaps more important than the nutrient effects. Soil structure may be as important to fertility as is its complement of nutrients. Soil aggregation or crumb tendency as promoted by humus improves the air-water relationship of soil, thus increasing the water retention capacity, and encouraging more extensive development of root systems of plants. Aggregation of soil particles is brought about by cellulose esters (cellulose acetate, methyl cellulose, and carbomethyl cellulose) resulting from bacterial metabolism (55). Other beneficial effects of bacterial metabolism associated with humus include an increased ability of the soil to absorb rapid changes in acidity and alkalinity, and the neutralization of certain toxic substances.

CHEMICAL COMPOSITION

While qualitatively the chemical composition may be fairly similar from one compost to another, inasmuch as organic matter is the substrate; quantitatively the variation will be great. The variability is due to differences in type or combinations of types of material being composted. In one instance the material may have a high nitrogen (low C/N) content; while in another, nitrogen may verge on being limiting. The gamut of trace elements also varies. Mixed municipal refuse may have a wider range of trace metals than would a particular crop or manure. Unfortunately, the broad array of metals in the municipal refuse may include a metal or toxic substance of public health significance. Some idea of the chemical analyses of typical composts may be gained from the information listed in Table III.

In general, compost has a nitrogen-phosphorus-potassium (NPK) content not high enough to permit it to be designated a fertilizer in the legal sense. Therefore, unless fortified with one or all of the three elements, it cannot be legally sold as a fertilizer. The usual designation is "soil conditioner." The legal NPK requirement for fertilizer varies from state to state; while the federal government has its own minimum for interstate shipment.

Applications

CROPS

For crop production, compost may be used both as mulch and as a soil conditioner. As a mulch, it has many of the characteristics of peat moss and bark. The advantages of utilizing compost as a mulch in comparison with the use of peat moss or bark, is that the compost when eventually incorporated into the soil releases absorbed water much more readily than does peat moss, and imposes a lesser demand on soil nitrogen than does bark. While peat moss may have a high water-holding capacity than does compost, the tenacity with which it clings to the water renders the water of little use to the crop plants being produced.

The C/N ratio of the compost is an important determinant of its immediate utility in crop production. If the C/N ratio is too high, i.e., above 20:1, the danger of nitrogen "robbing" becomes imminent. Nitrogen robbing is manifested by stunted growth and a chlorotic condition of the higher plants making up the crop being cultivated. It arises from the competition for nitrogen between the bacteria decomposting the compost and the roots of the crop plants. The bacteria being more efficient in assimilating the nitrogen, obtain the major portion of the available nitrogen, and thus in effect "rob" the higher plants. The nitrogen robbing effect can be avoided by applying sufficient nitrogen to the soil to compensate for any deficiency. This nitrogen "robbing" explains why crop production may actually drop when compost is first applied. However, even were no nitrogen added, the problem will disappear within a year.

The effect of compost, especially composted municipal refuse, on plant growth has been the subject of extensive study both in the U.S. and in Europe. Among the reports are those by Shinn (56), Sanderson and Martin (57), Sanderson (58), Hortenstine (59), and Hasler (60). Space does not permit detailed reportage of all of the studies, and hence only a few of the more recent ones are summarized here. In general, it might be stated that regardless of species of plant, growth was always enhanced by the addition of compost to a greater degree than by mineral fertilizers alone —provided of course, that a proper C/N ratio was maintained in the soil receiving compost. One of Hortenstine's findings that adds a new dimension to the usefulness of compost is that nitrification in the soil is reduced almost to zero. This characteristic is of value in preventing the nitrate contamination of ground waters. He also noted that compost brought about a reduction of nematodes in soil.

A problem that could arise in the use of large amounts of compost in crop production is the accumulation of objectionable elements in the soil. For example, Hasler and

Zuber (60) write of refuse and refuse-sewage sludge composts in Switzerland that have boron concentrations of 1 to 30 ppm. They point out that the addition of 120 tons of compost per acre can be the equivalent of 11 kg of crystalline borax.

LAND RECLAMATION

The application of compost is the obvious solution to land reclamation in areas where the top soil has been lost due to strip mining. The problem in such areas is to stop erosion and to supply a substrate on which a plant cover can take hold. Compost would supply both needs very readily. A kindred type of reclamation is the protection of hillsides denuded of vegetation by fire. An unreported study conducted in the Los Angeles area involved the spraying of a very thick slurry of composted municipal refuse to which suitable grass seeds had been added, on burned over hills. When placed on the hillsides, the slurry dewatered to a state much like a papier maché. When the rains came, the seeds sprouted and together with the compost effectively prevented mudslides or erosion from taking place. Compost is also useful for retaining soil on highway cuts and other excavations.

A potential use for compost is the reclamation of lands covered with mining tailings, fly ash deposits, and various chemical sludges. Hortenstine showed that tailings from phosphate mining activities could be made to support a good growth of vegetation through the addition of compost.

Potential of Composting in Waste Management

PRESENT STATUS

The present status of composting in solid waste management in the U.S. is far from promising, and the situation in Europe is not much better. In the U.S. when composting was at its peak, only a tiny fraction of the total wastes (less than 1%) generated in the U.S. was processed by composting. Of course, this is not surprising, in view of the fact that even in 1970, less than 10% of the total U.S. dumps were operated as sanitary landfills. In Europe, where composting has always received favorable attention, the fraction of refuse being composted is only 1 or 2% (61), and outside of Holland, composting does not enter into the solid wastes management of any major city. The compost that is produced in Europe is used mainly in "luxury" agriculture, such as vineyards.

The reasons for the unsuccessful status of composting in terms of extent of practice are not the lack of utility of the product nor of technology, but the unfavorable economics when judged by today's short-horizon pragmatic standards. The unfavorable economics stem from the inherent expensiveness of the process and from the absence of a demand for the product. As stated in an earlier section, capital costs range all the way from about $5,000 per ton per day capacity to more than $20,000 per ton, depending on the size of the plant. Operating costs range from about $5.00 to $14.00 or $15.00 per ton—again depending upon the size of the operation. Roughly, these costs are not far removed from those for modern incineration, exclusive of the latest air pollution control equipment. In strictly "dollars and cents" terms, less is accomplished by composting than by incineration with respect to volume reduction of the wastes. With sound incineration procedures, the volume reduction is on the order of 90%; whereas with composting, it is on the order of 30 to 40% at the most. (When speaking of volume reduction, it should be remembered that the percentages given are those only of the organic or combustible fraction of the waste load, i.e., about 50 to 60% of the incoming wastes.) Moreover, an incinerator can be built on a more compact scale, and land requirements are less because little or no storage is required in an incineration operation.

In the heyday of composting, the sale of salvage plus the compost product was expected to pay for a substantial portion, if not all, of the cost of the undertaking. Unfortunately, the market never developed. To absorb the entire compost production were all municipalities or even a sizable number of them to engage in composting, the product would have to be used in large scale agriculture. Here is the crux of the problem. Large scale agriculture is not interested in distributing bulky materials over its cropland, whether it be for purposes of conditioning the soil or of fertilizing it, especially when inorganic (mineral) fertilizers can be applied by "crop dusting" techniques, or anhydrous ammonia by way of irrigation water. The large scale farmer even regards the manure produced on his holdings as a liability. The application of bulky fertilizer or conditioner requires more labor and machinery expenditure per unit of fertilizer value, than does that of inorganic fertilizer.

Another difficulty in marketing is its seasonality. The product can only be applied to cropland at the end of, or prior to, the growing season—not during the season. Consequently, provision must be made for storing the daily production of a plant for long periods of time. Yet another difficulty is that the product itself is not of a high quality unless it has undergone relatively expensive processing. The low monetary value of the product is another handicap. In most cases, the transportation costs exceed the monetary value of the product.

As a result of all of the aforementioned handicaps, practically every compost enterprise undertaken in the U.S. has failed. Only two or possibly three minor exceptions can be found. According to latest reports (1971), a small plant is operating at Elmira, New York. Two others which may be in operation are one at Gainesville, Florida, and another at Norman, Oklahoma. The production of none of the three plants exceeds 50 tons per day, when they are operating.

FUTURE

The unfavorable status of composting will be changed as the people become sufficiently environment conscious to demand that waste management include social and environmental benefits when evaluating the applicability of a given waste technology. Thus, McGauhey (62) sees a place for composting as one of becoming that of salvage of remaining organic resource values for the land in maintaining productivity. Other uses would be land reclamation, sludge "stabilization" or "conditioning," and recreational.

The vast acreage of land despoiled by strip mining is a waste of land resources both in terms of production and even of recreation. As stated in the section on Applications, land could be readily reclaimed through the liberal application of compost. In other areas, large expanses of land are rendered useless because they serve as receptacles for chemical sludges which respond to no manner of treatment. Where compost has been tried as a means of stabilizing these sludges, the results have been favorable. More study is needed to determine the range of sludges amenable to the treatment and techniques for accomplishing the treatment.

In all of the potential applications, no monetary return is involved. In fact, not only would there be no cash return, but there would be actual expenditures because of transportation and application costs. However, the long term benefits more than make up for the costs involved.

The fallacy of judging the success of a compost operation in terms of its money-making record is a misconception that has always plagued composting, and is one that must be corrected. Thus, if the product cannot be sold, and a deficit results in terms of operational and capital costs, the entire enterprise is regarded as a failure—regardless of how well the plant may have operated. Yet, no one expects an incineration operation to earn money. Since composting also is a method for treating wastes, its success should be judged on the basis of performance and not on amount of profit.

The consensus at present is that composting will find its niche as regional management becomes the order of the day. When this time comes, agricultural waste disposal will become a public responsibility to a much greater extent than at present. Most of these wastes are readily composted with municipal refuse. Furthermore, because the area of land as available sites for wastes burial is rapidly diminishing and therefore must be used at maximum efficiency, and as air quality standards become stricter to a point at which air pollution control becomes so expensive as to rule out incineration, the only technology available for solid wastes processing will be composting. In fact, many cities are already taking the first step required, namely grinding—albeit they grind wastes solely to extend the life of a landfill site.

PART VI.

Home Composting

Home Composting According to the University of California Method

This section is devoted to "home composting," i.e., composting by the householder at his residence, because of the growing concern of many individuals about returning to the soil the plant nutrients contained in domestic refuse. This concern may derive from an overall interest in the environment or in "protecting the ecology," or it may arise simply from the home gardener's desire for an inexpensive source of compost for his home garden.

The first problem confronting the prospective composter is the finding of sound and comprehensible information on the subject. Many of the existing "how to's," "recipes," and directions are the products of hearsay, folklore, or legend. The result is that the novice composter is left confused, discouraged, or overly optimistic—depending upon the particular circular he or she may have read; or he or she is persuaded to make the undertaking more complicated than it need be. A second problem often met by the uninitiated is the complaint of neighbors that his compost pile stinks. The outcome of the latter usually is an ukase from the local health authority banning any further compost activity.

This section is written with the hope of providing the information needed to forestall the pitfalls mentioned in the preceding paragraph. It will not supply all of the answers, simply because conditions vary from place to place. However, it will give the reader pointers or clues as to the conduct of individual experimentation to find the method best suited to his situation.

GENERAL REQUIREMENTS

To conduct a successful compost operation, certain general or basic requirements must be met. Raw material of the proper composition and in a suitable physical condition must be provided. For an efficient operation, a minimum volume of raw material must be processed at a given time. In the method to be described, a bin is needed to contain the composting material. Finally, an appropriate procedure must be followed in setting up and conducting the compost operation. To be emphasized is the fact that no inoculums are needed. (See the preceding sections for an explanation of why inoculums are not needed.)

Descriptions and discussion of these major requirements constitute the subject matter for the remainder of this section.

RAW MATERIAL

It should be remembered that composting is a biological process; and hence that it is limited by the constraints that beset any biological activity. One of the principal factors in biological activity is the availability of essential nutrients. As pointed out in the preceding sections, these essential nutrients include carbon, nitrogen, phosphorus, and trace elements. Not only must they be present, but they also must be present in a form available to the microorganisms involved in composting. In other words, they must be present as compounds that the organisms can use. An anthropomorphic analogy would be the feeding of sawdust and urea to humans. The two materials contain carbon and nitrogen —but they would be of no nutritional value to the human subject.

Specifically, appropriate materials for composting are garden debris, manures, garbage, vegetable trimmings, unprinted paper and cardboard, and various absorbent materials. In other words, any decomposable organic material is suitable. (Exceptions for reasons of public health are human feces, diseased animals, plant debris heavily dosed with pesticides, and toxic material in general.) *Carbon-*

Nitrogen Ratio (C/N): A nutritionally related requirement generally unknown to the non-microbiologist, is that
carbon and nitrogen must be present in certain proportions.
The limiting ratio is usually the maximum one—in this case
from 25 to 30 to 1; i.e., 25 to 30 parts of carbon to 1 of
nitrogen. Too high a C/N ratio slows the process; whereas
too low a C/N ratio leads to a nitrogen loss in the form
of ammonia. The reasons were given in an earlier section.

For home composting, the C/N requirement can be met
by adjusting the proportion of "green" garden debris or of
garbage to "dry" garden debris. Examples of green garden
debris are lawn clippings, green leaves, green plant stems,
roots, flowers, etc. Dry debris refers to dried (no longer
green) grass (hay), matured flower stalks, branches (ex-
cluding leaves), straw, etc. The green material is rich in
nitrogen—and hence increasing the ratio of "greens" to
"drys" lowers the C/N ratio. The C/N ratio can be lowered
through the use of manures. Poultry manure is the most
effective because of its high nitrogen content. Dog feces
would also be a good source of nitrogen. Meat scraps are
rich in nitrogen—but who can afford to have meat scraps?

One may wonder how he can determine the C/N ratio
of his raw material. Unfortunately, determining the C/N
ratio involves the conduct of some exacting and expensive
tests. Consequently, some trial-and-error coupled with good
judgment are necessary. A useful way to assure an adequate
ratio is to follow the old Indore method in setting up the
pile, i.e., layering. Dry layers are alternated with "green"
or moist layers. Each layer is from 2 to 4 inches in depth.

The dry material is used for absorbing the excess moisture,
as well as to impart structural strength to the pile. It keeps
the pile "porous" and prevents compaction. Observation
tells us that sawdust, straw, and dried leaves are ideal materials for the purpose. Paper is not useful as an absorbent
because it becomes soggy and compacts.

Other materials that are useful or even required, are
phosphorus, and an array of trace elements. Generally these
substances are present in sufficient quantity in plant debris
and manures.

Some publications on home composting call for the addition of lime to keep the pile from becoming too acid in its reaction. In scientific terminology, this means that the lime is added to raise the pH of the pile—i.e. makes it turn from acid to alkaline. The reasoning is that most microorganisms cannot thrive under acid conditions or may even be killed. Actually, the ideal pH level for most microorganisms is 7.0, a level that corresponds to "neutrality." At pH 7.0, a material is neither "acid" nor "alkaline." This author has found that while most piles become somewhat acid during the onset of decomposition, this condition was not detrimental, nor did it last for a very long period of time. The trouble with adding lime is that it promotes the loss of nitrogen. The reasons are straightforward. The lime brings about a rise in pH to alkaline levels. At alkaline levels, the ammonium radical leaves its ionized state and is volatilized—it becomes a gas. Combining this volatilization with the high temperatures characteristic of an actively composting mass leads to an extensive loss of nitrogen in the form of ammonia. It must be admitted, however, that the addition of lime is followed by an improvement in the physical appearance and an ease in handling of the composting material.

MINIMUM VOLUME

Under the conditions prevailing in the San Francisco Bay area, the minimum recommended volume is one cubic yard. There is nothing of magic about the dimension one cubic yard. It simply is the minimum volume at which a pile becomes sufficiently self-insulating to retain its heat. Undoubtedly, in the Dakotas in midwinter, a three cubic yard pile may prove to be too small! The cubic yard volume is a convenient one for home composting because the amount is neither too unwieldy nor overwhelming, nor so tiny as to seem "piddling" to the gardener.

The home composter need not wait until he has accumulated a cubic yard of wastes from his own grounds. He can "borrow" debris from his neighbors, obtain vegetable trimmings from the local supermarket, or purchase a couple of sacks of steer manure. The manure not only provides a source of nitrogen, it also serves as an excellent absorbent.

If the volume is built up through accumulation, then care should be taken to turn the material occasionally in the manner to be described later. Otherwise, odor and fly problems may be encountered.

THE BIN

The bin may be constructed of concrete, wood, or even of hardware cloth. The minimum floor dimensions should be 3 ft x 3 ft. The height can be from 4 to 6 ft. It should be constructed such that one side can be removed to provide easy access to the composting material. If hardware cloth is used, the mesh size should be 1/4 inch and the "wire" should be of heavy gauge. Obviously, the "cloth" should be attached to a sturdy frame. An advantage in the use of hardware cloth is that all surfaces of the composting material are exposed to air. Disadvantages are: 1. The same exposure becomes a severe detriment if a fly problem should arise; 2. the life-span of such a bin will not be as long as that of a concrete or wooden bin; and 3. in a cold climate or in a windy area, little protection is had against heat loss.

A workspace equal to two or three times that of the floor space of the bin should be provided in front of the bin. This space is needed for turning the material. Another consideration is that of constructing a double bin. The twin bins can have a common wall, i.e. in effect a double-sized bin divided into two by a center partition. Material could be accumulated in one bin, while material in the second bin is composting.

To allay the qualms of local health authorities, the top surface (the exposed surface) should be covered with a fly-proof screen.

PROCEDURE

Preparation of Raw Material: If manure, or sawdust, or leaves, or dry grass is used as the absorbent; and vegetable trimmings, garden debris, lawn trimmings, and kitchen garbage as the nitrogen source, very little preparation of raw material is needed. For ease of handling, it would be advisable to chop up long or thick flower stalks (e.g. dahlias, marigolds, etc.) and vegetable stalks (corn, kale, pea vines, etc.) into pieces about 6 or 8 inches long. The chopping can be done with a sharp spade. Straw should be chopped into 3- or 4-inch pieces. While shredding the material with a power shredder would be ideal, it is not necessary. In the University experiments on "backyard" composting, excellent results were obtained without recourse to shredding.

As stated earlier, when starting a compost run, the material should be layered in the bin such that absorbent layers alternate with "wet" layers. The height of the pile should not exceed 6 feet. If the pile is too high, the material tends to compact and thereby exclude the necessary air from between the particles.

Moisture Content: Generally, if vegetable trimmings, lawn clippings, or kitchen garbage are used, the initial moisture content of the material will be adequate for composting. A good rule-of-thumb to follow is that the material is sufficiently moist if the surface of the particles glistens. An insufficiency of moisture will be manifested by the failure or delay of the material to "heat-up." An excess of moisture is soon revealed by the development of a foul odor and a drop in heating. The moisture content can be raised by sprinkling with tap water. A condition of excessive moisture can be remedied by adding more absorbent material or by increasing the frequency of turning to once-a-day.

Turning (Aeration): Inasmuch as the reasons for turning the material were given in an earlier section, only the technique is given at this time.

To begin the turning procedure, the front of the bin is removed. Then the contents of the bin are taken out, beginning with the top. Care should be taken to keep track of the position of the material in the bin so that when it is returned, that material which constituted the outer layers of the mass end up in the interior of the reconstituted pile. In short, the turning should be such that every particle in the original pile is at some time in the interior of the pile.

When transferring the material to and from the pile, it should be "fluffed" to insure maximum porosity in the pile. During the course of the first turning and thereafter, materials in the absorbent and wet layers should be mixed. In other words, the layering of "wet" and "dry" materials is discontinued with the first turning.

This author has found the five-tined pitchfork to be an excellent tool for turning.

Frequency of turning is a function of the composter's ambition, moisture content of the pile, and the urgency with which the finished compost is desired. The more frequent the turning (up to once-a-day), the faster the material composts. This author was able "to compost" a mixture of dry leaves (Sycamore), vegetable trimmings, and garden debris (total volume—1 cu yd) in 12 days under the following schedule: 1. First turning on the third day after starting the pile; 2. second turning on the third day after the first turning (i.e. skip a day); 3. and a third and final turning on the ninth day after setting up the pile. Composting was complete by the 12th day.

Monitoring the Process: The best way to monitor the process is by noting the course of the temperature. This can be done by purchasing a hotbed thermometer and using it to check the temperature inside the pile. The temperature inside the pile (about 12 to 15 inches from the surface) should rise to 110°F to 120°F within 24 to 48 hours after starting the process. It should reach 130°F and higher within 3 or 4 days after the start. Thereafter the temperature will remain at 130°F or higher until all of the readily decomposable material is stabilized. Then, the temperature will drop. When it drops to around 110°F, the material is ready for use.

Trouble-Shooting: If the temperature does not rise, or if it drops suddenly, the pile may be too wet, too dry, or the C/N ratio is too high. If the moisture content is too high, as stated earlier, the material will stink. If it is too low, the material will have a dry appearance. If the C/N ratio is too high, no odor will be noticeable, and the material will glisten if the moisture content is satisfactory.

The remedies for each of these problems were given in the preceding paragraphs.

Indore Method: For the less ambitious, the Indore method of composting is the suitable one for home composting. The paragraphs which follow are taken from an article written by this author in 1955.[1]

"The Indore method derives its name from the region of India in which it was developed. Composting according to this method involves a minimum of effort. In this procedure, layers of straw or dry, coarse material are alternated with manure or green organic matter. The mixture is placed either in open piles or in pits. The composting mass may be turned or left undisturbed. Turning the mass hastens decomposition. In either case the material should be covered with a two-inch layer of thoroughly compacted soil to prevent fly production and reduce odors. If the mass is turned, the first turning should be eight to ten days after placing the material. The second should occur thirty to forty days thereafter. The compost should be ready for use about a month later. If not turned, composting usually requires a year. Most farm and garden journal methods are modifications of the Indore process. The process is almost entirely anaerobic and therefore *does not generate sufficient heat to kill undesirable organisms already present.* (Emphasis added.)

Composting garden and kitchen waste according to the Indore method is best done in pits or bins. If space permits, a pit some 5' x 3' x 2' deep may be dug in the garden area. The pit is then filled with layers of lawn clippings, weeds, and garden refuse. This may be done gradually, taking care to cover each fresh addition with a layer of soil. Once the pit is filled it should remain undisturbed until the following year at which time the humus may be removed and used. If a tightly constructed bin is used, the same procedure holds with the exception that it should be approximately five feet high. In addition to covering with soil, it is advisable to keep the bin tightly screened on top to prevent access of flies to the interior of the bin. . . .

[1] Golueke, C. G. "Composting Farm and Garden Wastes", *California Vector Views,* 2(12):58-64 (December 1955).

Treatment of farm manure and farm waste products according to the Indore method is similar to that given for garden refuse, but using a larger pit or bin. Open piles or windrows may be used when large volumes are involved, but they should be immediately covered with a two-inch tightly compacted layer of soil to prevent fly production.

PART VII.

References
Definitions
and Comments

References

1. Waksman, S. A. *Soil and the Microbe,* New York, 1951.
2. Golueke, C. G., B. J. Card, and P. H. McGauhey. "Evaluation of Inoculums in Composting." *Applied Microbiology,* 2(1):45, 1954.
3. McGauhey, P. H., and C. G. Golueke. *Reclamation of Municipal Refuse by Composting.* Tech. Bull. No. 9, Sanit. Eng. Research Lab., Univ. of Calif., Berkeley, June 1953.
4. Weststrate, W. A. G. "The New Dutch Scheme for Refuse Disposal." *Public Cleansing and Salvage, 41:* 332, 1951.
5. Straub, H. "Die Herstellung von Kompost aus Abwasserschlamm und Hausmüll von Stadtbaurat." Berichte der Abwassertechnischen Vereinungen c. V. Die Stuttgarter Tagung. R. Oldenbourg, Munich, 1950.
6. Adams, R. C., F. S. Maclean, J. K. Dixon, F. M. Bennett, G. L. Martin, and R. C. Lough. "Second Interim Report of the Interdepartmental Committee on Utilization of Organic Wastes." *New Zealand Engineering,* 6:12, 1951.
7. Van Vuren, J. P. J. *Soil Fertility and Sewage.* Faber and Faber, Ltd., London, 1949.
8. Strauch, D. "Further Hygienic Investigations of the Influence of 'Promoting or Stimulating Factors' on Decontamination of Refuse and Sewage Sludge Components." International Research Group on Refuse Disposal. Information Bulletin No. 25. From *Translations of Bulletins 21-31* distributed by U.S. Public Health Service, Dept. H.E.W., 1969.
9. Gilbert, A. "Uber *Actinomyces thermophiles* und andere Actinomyceten." *Ztsehr. Hyg.,* 47:382, 194.
10. Miehe, H. *Die Selbsterhitzung des Heues.* Jena G. Fischer, 1907.
11. Forsyth, W. G. C. and D. M. Webley. "Microbiology: II. A Study of the Aerobic Thermophilic Bacteria Flora Developing in Grass Composts." Proceedings of the Society for Applied Microbiology, 1948.

12. Gray, K. "Research on Composting in British Universities." *Compost Science—Journal of Waste Recycling,* 11(5):12, 1970.
13. Regan, R. W., and J. S. Jeris. "A Review of the Decomposition of Cellulose and Refuse." *Compost Science,* 11:17, January–February 1970.
14. "Second Interim Report of the Interdepartmental Committee on Utilization of Organic Wastes." *New Zealand Engineering, 6* (Nos. 11-12) November-December 1951.
15. Wyley, J. S. "Progress Report on High-Rate Composting Studies." Engineering Bulletin, Proceedings of the 12th Industrial Wastes Conference, Series No. 94, May 1957.
16. Schulze, K. L. "Aerobic Decomposition of Organic Waste Materials (Continuous Thermophyllic Composting) Final Report," Michigan State Univ., Lansing, Mich., April 1961.
17. Allen, M. B. "The Thermophilic Aerobic Sporeforming Bacteria." *Bact. Reviews, 17:*125, 1953.
18. Golueke, C. G. "Temperature Effects on Anaerobic Digestion of Raw Sewage Sludge." *Sewage and Industrial Wastes* (presently *Journal of Water Pollution Control Federation*), 30:1225, October 1958.
19. "Investigation of Composting as a Means for Disposal of Fruit Waste Solids. Part II." Progress Report, National Canners Assoc. Research Foundation, Washington, D.C., August 1964.
20. Schulze, K. L. "Rate of Oxygen Consumption and Respiratory Quotients During the Aerobic Decomposition of a Synthetic Refuse." *Compost Science, 1:*36, Spring, 1960.
21. Schulze, K. L. "Relationship between Moisture Content and Activity of Finished Compost." *Compost Science, 2:*32, Summer 1961.
22. Pöpel, F. "Effects of Moisture and Oxygen Contents on Refuse Composting." International Research Group on Refuse Disposal. English Translation by U.S. Dept. H.E.W., IRGR Information Bulletin 13, December 1961.
23. Chrometzka, P. "Determination of the Oxygen Requirement of Maturing Composts." International Research

Group on Refuse Disposal, Information Bulletin No. 33, August 1968.

24. Lossin, R. D. "Compost Studies: Part III. Measurement of the Chemical Oxygen Demand of Compost." *Compost Science, 12*:31, March–April 1971.

25. Niese, G. "Experiments to Determine the Degree of Decomposition of Refuse by its Self-Heating Capability." International Research Group on Refuse Disposal, Information Bulletin No. 17, May 1963.

26. Rolle, G. and E. Orsanic. "A New Method of Determining Decomposable and Resistant Organic Matter in Refuse and Refuse Compost." International Research Group on Refuse Disposal, Information Bulletin No. 21, August 1964.

27. Möller, F. "Oxidation-Reduction Potential and the Hygienic State of Compost from Urban Refuse." International Research Group on Refuse Disposal, Information Bulletin No. 32, August 1968.

28. Obrist, W. "Enzymatic Activity and Degradation of Matter in Refuse Digestion: Suggested New Method for Microbiological Determination of the Degree of Digestion." International Research Group on Refuse Disposal, Information Bulletin No. 24, September 1965.

29. Lossin, R. D. "Compost Studies." *Compost Science, 11*:16, November-December 1970.

30. Howard, Albert. "The Waste Products of Horticulture and their Utilization as Humus." *Sci. Horticulture, 3*:213, 1935.

31. Ayyar, K. S., Viswanatha. *Symposium on the Utilization of Waste Products: Utilization of Farm Wastes. Madras Agricultural Journal, 21*:335, 1933.

32. Duthie, D. W. "Studies in Tropical Soils: IV. Organic Transformations in Soils, Composts, and Peat." *Journal Agr. Sci., 27*:162, 1937.

33. Howard, A. "The Manufacture of Humus by the Indore Process." *Journal Royal Society of Arts, 84*:25, 1935.

34. Baniface, A. "The Beccari Plant at Scarsdale, N.Y." *News and Water Works, 76*:75, 1929.

35. Beccari, G. Patent, U.S. 1,329,105, *Apparatus for Fermenting Garbage,* January 27, 1920. Reissue No. 15, 417, July 25, 1922.

36. Hyde, C. G. "The Thermophilic Digestion of Municipal

Garbage and Sewage Sludge, with Analogies." *Sewage Works Journal,* 4:993, 1932.

37. University of California. *Composting for Disposal of Organic Refuse.* Technical Bull. No. 1, Sanit. Eng. Research Lab., Univ. of Calif., Berkeley, 1950.

38. Eweson, E. Patent, U.S. 2,178,818. *A Digester with Superposed Chambers for Conversion of Organic Wastes Such as Garbage, Etc. by Bacterial Action.* November 7, 1939.

39. Wiley, J. S. "Composting Studies II. Progress Report on High-Rate Composting Studies." Purdue Univ. Engineering Bulletin, Proceedings of the 12th Industrial Waste Conference, Lafayette, Ind., 1957.

40. Maier, P. P. "Composting Studies I. Composting Municipal Refuse by the Aeration Bin Process." Purdue Univ. Engineering Bulletin Series No. 94, Proceedings of the 12th Industrial Waste Conference, Lafayette, Ind. 1957.

41. Wylie, J. C. "Composting." *Public Cleansing and Salvage,* 41:495, November 1951.

42. Hart, S. A., W. J. Flocker, and G. K. York. "Refuse Stabilization in the Land." *Compost Science,* 11(1):4, January–February 1970.

43. Stovoroff, R. P. "Capitalizing on Municipal Wastes by Composting." Paper presented at the Annual Meeting of the American Society of Civil Engineers, New York, October 1953.

44. Wiley, J. C. "An Approach to Municipal Composting." *Compost Science,* 2:6, Summer, 1961.

45. "Composting of Municipal Solid Wastes in the United States" Publication SW-47r, U.S. Environmental Protection Agency, Cincinnati, Ohio, 1971.

46. Kupchick, G. "The Economics of Composting Municipal Refuse." *Public Works,* 97:127, September 1966.

47. Harding, C. E. "Recycling and Utilization." *Compost Science,* 9:4, Spring 1968.

48. Blair, M. R. "The Public Health Importance of Compost Production in the Cape." *Public Health* (Johannesburg, South Africa), 15:70, 1952.

49. "The Agricultural Use of Sewage Sludge and Sludge Composts." Tech. Communication No. 7. Memorandum by the Agricultural Research Council Conference on

Sewage Sludge and Composts. London, England, Ministry of Agriculture and Fisheries, 1948.

50. Golueke, C. G. and H. B. Gotaas. "Public Health Aspects of Waste Disposal by Composting." *American Journal of Public Health,* 44(3):339, March 1954.

51. Banse, H. J., G. Farkasdi, K. H. Knoll, and D. Strauch. "Composting of Urban Refuse." International Research Group on Refuse Disposal, Information Bulletin No. 38, May 1968.

52. Knoll, K. H. "Composting from the Hygienic Viewpoint." International Research Group on Refuse Disposal, Information Bull. No. 7, July 1959.

53. "Progress Report." Unpublished Report, Joint USPHS–TVA Composting Project. Johnson City, Tenn., 1969.

54. Morgan, M. T. and F. W. Macdonald. "Tests Show MB Tuberculosis Doesn't Survive Composting." *Journal of Environmental Health,* 32:101, July–August 1969.

55. Quastel, J. H. "Influence of Organic Matter on Aeration and Structure of Soil." *Soil Science,* 73:419, 1952.

56. Shinn, A. F. "The Use of Municipal-Waste Compost for Growing White Clover on Calcareous Clay Soil in Tennessee." *Compost Science,* 11:13, July–August 1970.

57. Sanderson, K. C. and W. C. Martin, Jr. "Influence of Peat and Sewage Treated Garbage Compost-Amended Media on the Growth of Two Flowering Groups of Snapdragons." *Report on Research Results for Flower Growers–Snapdragon Studies, 1966-70.* Horticulture Series No. 15, Agricultural Experiment Station, Auburn Univ., Auburn, Alabama, September 1970.

58. Sanderson, K. C. "Herbicide Mulch Keeps Down Weeds in Ornamentals," in *Highlights of Agricultural Research,* 1970.

59. Hortenstine, C. G. "Effects of Garbage Compost on Soil Processes." Summary Progress Report submitted to the Bureau of Solid Waste Management, U.S. Dept. H.E.W., P.H.S., November 30, 1970.

60. Hasler, A. and R. Zuber. "Effect of Boron in Refuse Compost." International Research Group on Refuse Disposal, Information Bull. No. 27, August 1966.

61. Hart, S. A. "Solid Wastes Management–European Activ-

ity and American Potential." Final Report U.S.P.H.S., Dept. H.E.W., December 1967.

62. McGauhey, P. H. "American Composting Concepts." Public. No. SW-2r, Bureau of Solid Waste Management, U.S. Dept. H.E.W., 1969.

Definitions

Genus: In biology, the terms genus refers to a classification of plants, animals, or microorganisms with common distinguishing characteristics. "Genus" is a main subdivision of a family, and contains one or more species.

Attenuated: means weakened from continued growth under laboratory conditions. In the manuscript, it means weakened to the extent that the cultured organisms are at a competitive disadvantage with the indigenous "native" organisms. For pathogens, it means loss of virulence.

Facultative: Facultative aerobic organisms are those organisms capable of growing under aerobic and anaerobic conditions. "Obligate" aerobes can grow only in the presence of oxygen.

Fungi: Filamentous or single-celled cryptogamous ("primitive") plants which have discrete nucleus and a protoplasmic vacuole and lack chlorophyl.

Actinomycetes: Higher forms of bacteria characterized by a filamentous form of growth much like that of fungi, but lacking a discrete nucleus and a vacuole.

Kjeldahl Method: A standard method of determining a total nitrogen content of a substance by "digesting it" and distilling off the nitrogen, which is then measured.

Moisture content: Weight of water lost when a known amount of material is dried at a temperature of 120°C (+ a few degrees) for 8 hours or more. It usually is expressed as a percentage of the "wet" weight (dry wt. + wt. of water).

Redox potential: Relative oxidation effect of

oxidants in a solution measured as a comparative *Chaetomium gracile*: A filamentous fungus. electron pressure and expressed in volts.

Suboidal: Resembles trapeyoidal, but with rounded juncture of top and sides instead of angles (loaf-shaped).

Chloratic: Chlorophyll is damaged or not adequate—results in pale green or yellowish color. Symptomatic of nutrient deficiency and of some plant diseases. (Analogous to paleness in humans.)

Nitrification: Conversion and oxidation of organic-nitrogen to nitrite and nitrate brought about by the activity of certain types of bacteria.

Nematodes: A group of worms in the *Nemathelminthe*-elongated, cylindrical, unsegmented worms. Some are plant parasites, some human parasites (pinworm, hookworm) and some are free-living.

Comments

(a) Reconciling Chrometzka's findings with Schulze's results: Schulze:

1) 20,000 cu ft/ton/dayr915 cu ft/ton/hr.
2) 915 cu ft/ton/hrr2.59 × 10^8 mm^3/ton/hr.
3) 2.59 × 10^8mm^3/ton/hrr129,564 mm^3/lb/hr.
4) 129,564 mm^3/lb/hrr285 mm^{3}air/gm/hr.
5) 285 mm^{3}air/gm/hrr51 mm^{3}o$_2$/gm/hr.

(air at 18% o$_2$). This is within Chrometzke overall range. Keeping aerobic conditions in a compost pile doesn't necessarily mean every particle is exposed to oxygen at all times. It means the avoidance of the *symptoms* of anaerobiosis, namely, bad odors.

(b) COD: Quoting Lossin: "We can measure the extent of biological oxidation in the system by measuring the extent to which the refuse (compost) is oxidized by chemical means. This ability to be oxidized is called the chemical oxygen demand or COD."

I doubt that Niese intended his tests to be anaerobic— hence the use of cotton wadding to plug the flasks. The fact that the material heated indicates that the material was not completely anaerobic.

Compost in cold climates: Compost piles will heat in the Northeast, provided they are shielded from high winds, and the dimensions of the piled compost is great enough— probably a minimum of 8 to 10 ft in cross section and 6 to 8 ft in height. Ground refuse has excellent insulation properties. The outer cold layer simply becomes a bit thicker. I don't know the answer for the sub-zero temperatures in Minnesota, the Dakota's, etc. They probably would heat up —but slowly! (I visited Minneapolis, Minn. in January and encountered temperatures of $-5°F$ to $-18°F$!)

Destruction of pathogens: Pathogens will not multiply in

the pile. High temperatures plus exposure to other organisms and their (i.e. other organisms) metabolic products combine to provide unfavorable conditions. Consequently, if some pathogens are not exposed to the high temperatures in the pile, they will not multiply. However, good public health practice dictates that exposure of the public to pathogens be kept at a minimum. Hence, the caution against using raw sewage sludge still holds. I worry about contamination of the finished compost with sludge that never even reaches the compost pile, as a result of "sloppy housekeeping."

TABLE III

CHEMICAL COMPOSITION OF VARIOUS COMPOSTS

Element	1[a]	2[b]	3[c] Sludge Added	3[c] No Sludge	4[d]
Carbon	38.3	23.51	33.07	32.89	—
Nitrogen	1.57	0.97	0.94	0.91	0.57
Potassium	0.40	0.21	0.28	0.33	0.22
Sodium	—	—	0.42	0.41	—
Calcium	—	—	1.41	1.91	1.88
Phosphorus	0.40	0.16	0.28	0.22	0.26
Magnesium	—	—	1.56	1.92	0.12
Iron	—	—	1.07	1.10	—
Aluminum	—	—	1.19	1.15	—
Copper	—	—	<0.05	<0.03	—
Manganese	—	—	<0.03	<0.05	24 ppm
Nickel	—	—	<0.01	<0.01	—
Zinc	—	—	<0.005	<0.005	606 ppm
Boron	—	—	<0.0005	<0.0005	33 ppm
Mercury	—	—	e	e	—
Lead	—	—	e	e	—

[a] Vegetable trimmings plus 16% (by weight) paper (12).
[b] Municipal refuse.
[c] Johnson City municipal refuse (46).
[d] Gainesville compost (municipal refuse).
[e] Not detected.

INDEX

compost (*cont.*)

composition of, 72, 103
"fresh," 31
grinding of, 46
as humus, 13, 71
land reclamation and, 74
nature and value of, 71–78
as soil conditioner, 13, 71–72
in waste management, 74–78

composting

aeration in, 31–33, 52–53, 86–87
aerobic, 13–14, 26
anaerobic fermentation in, 49
bacterial activity in, 39–40
biological nature of, 15–16
of cannery wastes, 59–61
carbon-nitrogen (C/N) ratio in, 23–24, 37, 41, 55–56, 72–74, 83
in cold climate, 101
color in, 42
constraints in, 15–16
costs in, 57–58
"decomposition" concept in, 15
defined, 13, 99–100
design considerations in, 56–57
double standard in, 6
duration of, 45
environmental factors in, 3, 15
European methods of, 5
failure of as business enterprise, 76
Fairfield Hardy digester for, 5–6
final processing and staging in, 46
fly larvae in, 65–68
future of, 76–78
genetic traits in, 32–33
grinding in, 38
health aspects of, 65–68
home, 81–89
inoculation in, 18–20
isolates in, 16–18
in late 1960's up to present time, 6–9
macronutrients in, 23
mass inoculation in, 20
maturation in, 45
mechanized, 38–46
mesophilic, 14
microbiology of, 16–22
in mid-1960's, 5–6
moisture content and control in, 26–27, 53
municipal wastes in, 1–4
night soil and, 1, 65, 68
during 1950–1960, 1–2
nitrogen-phosphorus potassium (NPK) content, 6–7
nutrient balance in, 23–25
nutritional requirements in, 8
odor in, 8, 14, 32, 42, 86
organic wastes in, 22–23
over-mechanization in, 4
oxygen uptake in, 31–32, 41
pathogenic organisms in, 2–3, 66–67, 101–102
physical appearance in, 40
plant nutrients and, 1–2
in pre-1950 period, 1
process description in, 38–41
progress since 1950, 1–9
rate controlling factors in, 25–33
research in, 2–3
sampling in, 43
soil improvement and, 2, 13, 71–72
as solid waste "disposal" method, 4
sorting in, 37–38
special applications in, 59–61
stabilization in, 41–45
steps in, 37–46